THE POETRY OF YŪNUS EMRE

The Poetry of Yūnus Emre,
A Turkish Sufi Poet

Grace Martin Smith

UNIVERSITY OF CALIFORNIA PRESS
Berkeley • Los Angeles • London

UNIVERSITY OF CALIFORNIA PUBLICATIONS IN MODERN PHILOLOGY

Volume 127

UNIVERSITY OF CALIFORNIA PRESS
BERKELEY AND LOS ANGELES, CALIFORNIA

UNIVERSITY OF CALIFORNIA PRESS, LTD.
LONDON, ENGLAND

Library of Congress Cataloging-in-Publication Data

Yunus Emre, d. 1320?
   [Poems. English]
   The poetry of Yūnus Emre / Grace Martin Smith.
       p.   cm. —(University of California publications in
modern philology ; v. 127)
   Includes bibliographical references.
   ISBN 0-520-09781-5 (pbk : alk. paper)
   1. Yunus Emre, d. 1320?—Translations into English. I. Title.
II. Series.
PL248.Y8A27 1993
894'.3511—dc20   93-12561
                                              CIP

To John

Contents

Acknowledgments

While working on this book I benefited from the help of many people and institutions, more than I can enumerate, but all of whom I wish most sincerely to thank. First and foremost I want to thank my husband John Masson Smith, Jr., for his support and help. The Translations Program of the National Endowment for the Humanities made possible the research and writing on this project; Dr. Susan Mango of the N.E.H. was of much assistance to me throughout. I am also most thankful for the help of the Süleymaniye Library (Istanbul) staff, and in particular of Muammer Ülker, the library's most knowledgeable director. Among those whose contributions I would especially acknowledge is the late Abdülbâki Gölpınarlı, who graciously contributed commentary that elucidates difficult points in the text and makes more accessible his special understanding of Yūnus's work. To be able to have a commentary by this well-known scholar of Yūnus's poetry—a learned man from the culture itself—is a valuable addition. I am particularly grateful, also, for the help and support of Samuel G. Armistead and James T. Monroe. Robert Dankoff and W. C. Hickman kindly agreed to read the manuscript, and made many useful corrections and suggestions, for which I am most thankful. Professor Doctor Günay Kut, as always, graciously and willingly provided a wealth of information. Nedret İşli managed to track down materials that I might otherwise never have found. To my old friend Gerry Oberling, I owe many debts of gratitude, the latest one for her meticulous editorial work. Ruth Cooper, and especially Johanna Movassat, patiently typed and retyped the manuscript; one could not wish for more helpful typists. Rose Anne White patiently supervised the final preparation of the manuscript, and Phyllis Brooks courageously and competently prepared the camera-ready copy.

Foreword

Yūnus Emre is often referred to as the national poet of the Turks, and, indeed, he has maintained his great popularity for six centuries. Yūnus is the most important representative of early Turkish mysticism; he can be considered the founder of the Alevī-Bektaşī literature, and his influence on later *tekke* poetry was enormous. Moreover, his *ilāhī*s (hymns) have played an important role in *ṣūfī* (Islamic mystic) ceremonies, especially among the Bektaşī order of dervishes. I hope that a translation of his poetic works will acquaint the non-Turkish reader with the art and thinking of one of Turkey's best loved and most significant poets. I also hope that this book will be helpful to students of Turkish (modern and Ottoman) and to all those interested in Islamic poetry and piety.

The Introduction outlines the historical, religious, literary, and linguistic background of Yūnus Emre and discusses his life and works. In Notes on Translation, I explain why I decided to base my translations on one relatively sound text, the Fatih manuscript, emending it where necessary in the light of other reliable texts. I selected poems primarily according to my evaluation of their artistic and especially their musical quality. In general I did not select poems that were solely didactic in tone or those filled with special religious terminology that would require word by word explanations. Nor did I select poems that were close copies, apparent variants, or fragments of other poems. I have provided a glossary of proper names, literary references, and Islamic and historical terms that need further clarification. There is also a selected bibliography of works on Yūnus Emre.

Introduction

HISTORICAL BACKGROUND

Yūnus lived during the late thirteenth and the beginning of the fourteenth century. His *Risāle (Treatise)* is dated 707/1307–8, and according to one historical register, he died in 720/1320–21 at the age of eighty-two. He lived, therefore, during one of the most turbulent periods of Anatolian history, one that began with catastrophe, yet, for Yūnus, ended in hope. The thirteenth and fourteenth centuries were the Mongol period. During the first sixty years of the thirteenth century, Chingis Khan and his three successors created an unmatched empire extending from China into central Europe and well into the Middle East. In 1230 a small Mongol army—of some thirty or forty thousand men—was sent to Azerbaijan to continue the process of Middle Eastern conquest begun during Chingis's Khwarezmian campaign of 1218–23. This army dislodged local Turkish nomads, who took refuge in Anatolia, and then came into conflict with the Turkish state of the Seljuks of Rūm in the Baba Ishak insurrection of 1239. In the early 1240s, the Mongols began to encroach directly upon the Seljuks, whose resistance led to a confrontation under the great mountain of Köse Dağ, near Suşehri in central Anatolia, in 1243. The undisciplined impetuosity of some Seljuk warriors gave the Mongols a success at the outset; then the timorous Seljuk sultan abandoned his strong defensive position on the mountain, his camp, and any hope of blocking the enemy's advance. The Mongols marched on into central Anatolia, sacking Sivas and killing all the men in Kayseri, as well as enslaving the women and children and forcing the Seljuks to become their vassals.

In 1256 a large Mongol army, led by Hülegü Ilkhān, arrived in the Middle East, with at least 150,000 men and their nomad families and domestic animals. Some 300,000 of these people were established in Azerbaijan, Transcaucasia, and eastern Anatolia to take advantage of the summer grazing in the highlands and the lowland winter pastures of the Kura and Aras valleys and of the Fertile Crescent in Iraq as far as Baghdad. Another 150,000 to 200,000 nomads were removed from Azerbaijan to central Anatolia, where they occupied winter quarters (*kışlaq*) on the dry plains extending beside and

1

below the Tuz Gölü. Akşehir, Aksaray, and Kırşehir are named as *kışlaq*s, and each may have supported a Mongol division (*tümen*) of 10,000 men with their families and herds. With the change of seasons, these nomads moved to summer pastures (*yaylaq*) in the adjacent mountains: the Sultan range behind Akşehir; the Melendiz, Ala, and Erciyaş mountains beyond Aksaray; and the uplands around Kırşehir. Farther east, another Mongol group was assigned to the region around Diyarbakir, and the nascent Karakoyunlu and Akkoyunlu may also have been migrating over eastern Anatolian routes, as they were to do later.

These "Mongols" were mostly Turkish in language. Inner Asian tribalism, unlike that of the Arabs and Africans, is ordered not by genealogical relations but by political attachment between tribesman and chief. There is no anomaly, therefore, in the idea of Turkish tribesmen with Mongol chiefs, and it is in fact the possibility of such relationships that made the Mongol Empire a reality. The success of the Mongols was as much a matter of recruitment—of the enlistment of a considerable part of the largely Turkish nomad population of Inner Asia—as of the better known conquests that this large scale recruitment made possible. The "Mongol" invasion of the Middle East was therefore in fact a second Turkish invasion, and a much larger one than the eleventh-century incursion that established the Seljuks in the area. The Seljuks brought with—or after—them some tens of thousands of Turks; the Mongols brought hundreds of thousands and created the substantial Turkish population from which, probably in considerable part because of the nomadic tendency to rapid population growth, the Turks developed into a major Middle Eastern people.

The adjustment of this population to its new Middle Eastern setting was a difficult and conflict-ridden one. The Mongol dynasty indulged in coups, rebellions, and succession struggles that affected not only the rulers, governors, and generals but also their supporters and soldiers and their families: the winners were able to despoil and displace the losers. The Seljuk vassals of the Mongols, in their turn, competed among themselves and occasionally and unsuccessfully plotted against the Mongols; the losers, great and small, again suffered. In a famous incident, the defeated Seljuk prince 'Izzuddīn Keykavūs had to emigrate with his followers to Byzantium. And the Turks who had been in the Middle East before the Mongols, and who had retreated steadily westward ahead of the Mongol advance insofar as they did not enlist as "Mongols," ended by establishing an arc of petty emirates or beyliks—Jandar, Osman (the Ottomans), Germiyan, Aydin, Saruhan, Menteşe, and Karaman, among others—in the north, west, and south of Anatolia around its solid Mongol center. These little states fought one another, attacked the Seljuks, rebelled against the Mongols, and, when their position made it possible, encroached upon Byzantium.

Around the turn of the thirteenth–fourteenth century much of this turmoil abated. The Mongol ruler Ghazan suppressed the tendency to succession struggle by exterminating much of the dynastic family; he also wrought a great improvement in the political and cultural climate by converting to Islam, along with his court and those of his Mongol army and people who were not already Muslims. He extended direct Mongol administration over Anatolia at the expense of the Seljuks (who faded away around 1307) and reformed Mongol government throughout the Middle East to promote a harmonious nomad-sedentary collaboration in place of the nomadic depredation and exploitation of the settled peoples that had characterized the first half-century of Mongol rule. Agriculture revived, revenues increased, royal and private patronage of the arts and architecture burgeoned within the Mongol realm, and the little Turkish states around its edges in Anatolia began to flourish modestly. In Yūnus's last years, Anatolia was verging on the lively and progressive condition that was so vividly recorded a little later by the great traveler 'Ibn Baṭṭūṭa. The Mongol elite was becoming educated and cultured. The Anatolian Turks were achieving self-government and religious autonomy through their *ahī* and *ṣūfī* organizations and were beginning to retrieve their military self-respect as *ġāzī*s. In 717/1317, about three years before the death of Yūnus, the young Mongol prince Abū Sa'īd came to the throne of the Middle Eastern empire to preside over "the best period of the domination of the Mongols."[1]

This large influx of Turks under Mongol leadership had, of course, cultural as well as social and political consequences. The Seljuk invasions had implanted Turkish government in the Middle East but not Turkish culture in any permanent way. The Turks who came with the Seljuks were few in number and most of them were illiterate nomads and soldiers; their oral arts and traditions, their unwritten music and the like, were given no permanent form. Only the Turkish rulers had some requirement for written records, and they obtained these from literate Persians, who wrote in Persian and Arabic. The Mongol invasion, however, produced a much larger and a much more complex Turkish society in Anatolia. More nomads were brought in, probably soon generating a population surplus that could not be supported by nomadism. The incoming nomads also displaced many of the nomads previously established in Anatolia (for instance, the Ottomans), depriving them of pastures and forcing them into nonnomadic occupations. Thus Turkish Anatolian society came to include not only nomads but farmers and town dwellers. And it was the Turkish merchants, craftsmen, clerics, administrators, and rulers—the *ahī*s, *ṣūfī*s, *'ulemā'* (learned and religious classes), and *ümerā'* (ruling class)—who developed the need and demand for the production of Turkish writing and literature.

LITERARY AND LINGUISTIC BACKGROUND

In his poetry, Yūnus refers to Mevlānā, that is, to Jelāleddīn Rūmī (d. 1273), who has been called the greatest mystic poet of all time. The Persian works of this poet, especially his *Meṣnevī* and *Dīvān-i Şams-i Tabrīzī*, have profoundly affected Turkish

---

1   Al-Ahri, *Ta'rikh-i Shaikh Uwais*, ed. and trans. J. B. Van Loon. (The Hague: Uitgeverij Excelsior, 1954), p. 51.

writers.[2] He was known primarily as a man of God who in later life became a fervent poet of Love, transformed by the mystical love attachment he formed with a strange, wild-looking, itinerant Turkish dervish named Şams-i Tabrīzī. This attachment turned the sober scholar into a distracted lover who poured out his affection and yearning in voluminous poetry, especially after he was separated from Şams and after Şams was killed by those jealous of Rūmī's attachment to him.

Rūmī's son Sulṭān Veled was of very meager artistic talents compared to his father: his works are mostly dry and didactic, lacking real poetic skill. The dominant purpose of his writing was to spread the message of his great father, and to do this he wrote in the current literary forms: didactic, mystical, and erotic-mystical. There were other poets who also wrote didactic religious poetry, such as Aḥmed Faqīh and Şeyyād Hamza, who stressed the impermanence of the world with all its delights and the horrors of the Final Judgment. In addition to didactic poetry, there were lyric works composed by Sulṭān Veled, Dehhanī, Şeyyād Hamza, 'Āşıq Paşa, and Gülşehrī. Narrative literature also began to flourish, treating a variety of subjects, some of the most popular of which were based on the life, military exploits, and miracles of the Prophet and of his son-in-law 'Alī.

When Jelāleddīn Rūmī wrote at the Seljuk court in Konya, he wrote in Persian, the language of the court and undoubtedly his own mother tongue. He did compose a few lines of mixed Persian-Turkish poetry, but this was probably just a matter of following a current poetic fashion. His son Sulṭān Veled, however unskilled he may have been as a poet, was extremely important for initiating the use in Anatolia of Turkish as a literary language, incorporating sixty-four Turkish verses into his *Ibtidā'nāme*, *Rebābnāme*, and *Dīvān*. Both the Turks and the Turkish language had been looked down upon at the Seljuk court, and it was not until the disintegration of Seljuk rule and the growth of Turkish principalities that Turkish as a literary language received official patronage.

YŪNUS EMRE

The literary pioneering by Sulṭān Veled, the expository versifier, helped make possible the accomplishment of the poet-preacher Yūnus: a large body of beautiful religious poetry in flowing Turkish that unites a fully developed poetic style and technique with all the fervor and urgency of the proselytizing holy minstrel, producing a religious message couched in, and enhanced by, a lovely, rhythmic poetry, much of which is still recited and sung today in Turkey, more than six hundred years after Yūnus "walked on to God."

Yūnus Emre is believed to have lived in Anatolia during the last part of the thirteenth and the beginning of the fourteenth century. At the end of his *Risāle* (*Treatise*), he wrote

---

2   Among those who have devoted much of their lives to studying Rūmī is R. A. Nicholson, editor of Rūmī's *Mes̱nevī*.

that he finished it in 707 (1307-8).[3] We know very little for certain about him. Many say he lived in Sarıköy in the Sakarya valley; some think he lived in Karaman, near Konya; and numerous other villages also claim possession of his grave. He shared with a number of saints and holy men the reputation of being illiterate (*ümmī*). This reputation, of course, would make his poetic achievement seem even more wonderful to the common folk and would also cause him to share a characteristic, at least in folk belief, with the Prophet, who some said was illiterate. But such a concept of the simple holy man—God's chosen one, untainted by worldly learning—is, we know, common to all religious traditions. Yūnus himself spoke disparagingly of *'ilm*, formal "book" learning, contrasting to it the superiority of *'irfān*, spiritual knowledge. However, the notion of his illiteracy has been successfully discounted and disproved, as far as I am concerned, by Abdülbâki Gölpınarlı, who points out Yūnus's considerable knowledge of the Islamic sciences and literatures, including Persian classical literature—the latter, at least, being something he could not have learned from strictly oral sources. Some have even argued that he must surely have attended a *medrese*, an Islamic college of higher education. But there is no direct evidence to support this.

I do agree with those who think that he was connected with a *tekke*,[4] perhaps living there, breathing the *tekke*'s religious atmosphere, performing his dervish duties (including missionary duties), attending the sheikh (spiritual leader), and participating in the dervish rituals and fellowships, which would have been enhanced by his songs and poems. It seems to me that, unless Yūnus had been a dervish himself, he could never have written poems and songs so knowledgeable about and so sympathetic with *tekke* life and thought and so closely responsive to the emotional and religious needs of the *tekke* congregations that they have been sung in *tekke*s down to the present.[5]

Another interesting and consequential aspect of Yūnus's life is his work as a proselytizing preacher. The important function of the dervishes in spreading Islam has

---

3   In a *mecmū'a* (manuscript with mixed contents) in the Bayezid Umumi Kütüphanesi, no. 7912, Adnan Erzi found a note saying that Yūnus died in the year 720/1320-21, and that the length of his life was eighty-two years (*Belleten*, Türk Tarih Kurumu, no. 53, January 1950).

4   Among those who believe Yūnus was associated with a *tekke* is the literary historian Nihad Sami Banarlı, who discusses Yūnus in his *Resimli Türk Edebiyati Tarihi* (Ankara: Milli Eğitim Bakanlığı, n.d.), fasc. 5, pp. 325-36. Religious orders sprang up in Anatolia as well as in the rest of the Muslim world. These orders were often founded on the teachings of an influential man of piety or charismatic personality who usually gave the order its name, such as the order of the Mevlevīs inspired by Mevlānā Jelāleddīn Rūmī. Men and women were attached to the order with varying degrees of closeness and assembled at buildings (*tekke*s, *dergāh*s, etc.), presided over by sheikhs, to pray and worship and participate in the special religious ceremonies and in the communal life centered upon the *tekke*. Those most closely associated with the *tekke*s—often through formal initiation—were called dervishes.

5   It would be exciting to learn if the actual musical accompaniment to the songs has remained essentially the same over six centuries.

often been remarked upon in the context of the Ottoman conquests in the Balkans and in Europe.[6]   Yūnus lived in an Anatolia politically dominated by the mostly Turkish-speaking Mongols.   It was a land filled with a variety of peoples: Byzantines, Turks, Mongols, Persians, and others.   The Islam of the relatively new Muslim arrivals, and perhaps also that of some who had accepted Islam a long time previously, was often superficial and error-filled.   Bertrandon de la Brocquière, traveling in Anatolia at the beginning of the fifteenth century, was told that the Ramazanoğlu bey, when people spoke to him of the two prophets Jesus and Muḥammad, said, "For my part, I am for the living prophets; they will be more useful to me than dead ones."[7] An incident told by Latīfī and ʿAlī, two literary historians, illustrates the latitudinous religious atmosphere of Anatolia, even considerably after the time of Yūnus, in the fifteenth century.   E. J. W. Gibb recounts it: "a popular preacher was one day discoursing in Brusa on the text of the Koran which runs, 'We make no difference between any of His apostles.'   This he interpreted to mean that all the Prophets were equal in degree. 'Wherefore,' he added, 'I esteem not Muhammad to be more excellent than Jesus—on the Twain be peace!'"[8]   An Arab who was in the audience was shocked by this liberal interpretation of the text and tried to get the preacher to recant.   The preacher would not, and moreover the people of Bursa sided with him.   The Arab returned home and procured a *fetva* (official opinion on a legal matter) demanding that the preacher recant. This the preacher never did, even though the Arab traveled seven times between his country and Bursa, bringing seven *fetva*s.   Yūnus's mission—self-imposed or set by his sheikh—was to travel among these people, inform and educate them concerning the basic Islamic tenets, and strengthen their faith.

Yūnus mentions that he has been to Azerbaijan and other, even less likely places, which are probably claimed only in a conventional poetic sense.   In one of his most delightful poems, evoking the atmosphere of rugged Anatolian conditions, as well as the feeling of a good, rousing *tekke* song, we can perhaps glimpse the life an itinerant preacher of the fourteenth century might have led (Poem CXLI):

Of the wine which flows from God, we have drunk; praise be to God!
We have crossed this great sea of power, praise be to God!
These mountains, oak forests, and vineyards opposite, with good health and peace
   of mind we have passed over; praise be to God! . . .

---

6   Ömer Lütfi Barkan was among the first to study this problem.   In my article "Some *Türbes/Maqam*s of Sarı Saltuq, an Early Anatolian Turkish *ğāzī*-Saint," *Turcica* 14 (1982), I treat the question of conversion and proselytizing.

7   Bertrandon de la Brocquière, *The Voyage d'Outremer*, trans. Galen R. Kline (New York: Peter Lang, 1988), p. 54.

8   *A History of Ottoman Poetry* (London: Luzac and Co., 1900; rpt. 1963); vol. 1, pp. 233–34.

> To the countries where we've gone, to those pure hearts [filled with affection],
> we have spread Tapduk's inner truth to the people; praise be to God!
> Come here and let's make peace, if you're a stranger, let's get acquainted. Our
> horses were saddled up, we rode out; praise be to God!
> We went down to Rūm[9] for the winter months, [where] we did much good and
> bad. Then when spring returned, we moved on; praise be to God!
> Spring by spring we collected together, we became a river; we flowed down into
> the sea, overflowed; praise be to God!

In this wonderful "hymn," with its great, stirring refrain "*el hamdu lillah*," Yūnus tells us about the life of a wandering preacher who has to travel long distances to spread the message of his sheikh or spiritual mentor (Tapduk). The countryside must have been filled with nomads who came in, as mentioned, with the Mongol armies. With them, he moves from summer pastures to wintering sites and speaks tantalizingly of having committed "much good and bad"—"good" perhaps being his spreading of Tapduk's message, "bad" perhaps meaning participation in raids with the tribes. Once again, we can only guess. Yet it does seem clear from this poem and others that he had a definite message to get across: he was deeply committed to teaching the basic principles of Islam as well as to singing his own gift of love.

Preaching is a sacred art, and Yūnus could draw upon a rich and vital tradition going back to such important religious figures as Aḥmed Yesevī (d. 1166). In fact, some of Yūnus's poetry resembles Aḥmed Yesevī's very much. Memorized poetry such as that recited by itinerant preachers formed a large part of the education of an essentially non-literate population. It promoted proper behavior, conveyed the basic Muslim message to potential converts, and strengthened the faith of all Muslims. Preachers edify with exemplary stories taken from the Kuran and *had īth* literature, as well as from traditional Islamic literatures.

From Yūnus's poetry, we know that a person named Tapduk was his spiritual master. Beyond this, we have only his poetic message, in which different people see different things. In modern Turkey he is claimed as the national poet, although when he lived there was no Turkish nation and the Ottomans were just beginning their enterprise. Now, of course, when he has been so enthusiastically embraced by the whole country, such a title acquires real significance.

Yūnus's message was couched in easy poetry, employing familiar meters and originally no doubt musical accompaniment. J. R. Walsh treats Yūnus as a hymnodist, and states that such hymnody, called *ilāhī*, seems to be found only in Asia Minor.[10] For his poetry, Yūnus used both classical, quantitative (*'arūż*) meters and syllabic

---

9   The designation Rūm at that time probably referred to central Anatolia.

10   "Yūnus Emre: A 14th-Century Turkish Hymnodist," *Numen* 7, fasc. 2-3 (December 1960), reprinted in *Yūnus Emre and His Mystical Poetry*, ed. T. S. Halman, Indiana University Turkish Studies 2 (Bloomington: Indiana University Press, 1981), pp. 111-26.

(*parmak hesābı*, reckoning by counting on the fingers) meters. As a practicing poet, he had a headful (heartful?) of meters to choose from when composing, and sometimes used one kind, sometimes another. The classical meters in his poetry are, quite naturally, those that best suit the Turkish *parmak hesābı* meters. In fact, it is often possible to read the same poem according to either metrical scheme. It is true, of course, that Yūnus's use of *'arūż* is less than perfectly in accord with classical usage, but he is in good company: some scholars of Persian literature point to Rūmī's "defective" use of *'arūż*!

Yūnus's poetry was, at least in part, composed orally. Ilhan Başgöz[11] points out that Yūnus uses certain verbs—*söylemek*, *çatmak*, and *soylamak*—which reveal the oral nature of his poetry. Moreover, *soy soylamak* indicates that the poetry was accompanied by music, another sign of oral composition. Başgöz also notes that Yūnus refers to himself as *'āşıq* (folk poet or minstrel), and *'āşıq* poetry is never recited without music. He goes on to say that the poetry that was not written in *'arūż* must have been oral. The fact that there are numerous metrical errors in the poems that can be read as *'arūż* may also indicate oral composition.

Yūnus's poetic vocabulary is filled with references to nature and the everyday life of Anatolia, as well as to traditional figures, the Kuran, and classical Persian literature and mythology. This rich and varied background, despite Yūnus's limited range of subjects, ensures that his poetry is always interesting. He is able to make lively use even of the tired tropes of classical literature; even the overworked nightingale gives good service in Poem CLV:

> I am a nightingale; I came singing. I came holding the royal patent on my
> tongue.
> I came here to sell my musk; I am a deer; my grazing place is There.

Some of Yūnus's most beautiful and powerful poetry is devoted to a description of nature, as in Poem VIII:

> I was going along the road; [I saw] a tree stretched tall. It was so charming, so
> sweet, my heart said, "Reveal a few secrets!"
> What sense is it to stretch [so] tall like this? Because this world is transitory.
> This is the mark of excessiveness; come here, pass over to humbleness.
> Adorning yourself so charmingly like this, and decorating yourself so sweetly, the
> heart stretching out to God—What is [your] wish? What do you need?
> Trees grow old, time passes; the bird alights [just] once on the branch. Birds
> have not alighted on you yet, neither dove nor francolin.

And again in Poem LXXI (not in the Fatih manuscript):

> Again you have overflowed, mad heart. Will you burble like the water? Again
> you have flowed, my bloody tears. Will you block my way[s]?

---

11 "The Human Dimension of Yūnus Emre's Transformation," *ibid.*, pp. 33–34.

What should I do? I can't reach the Beloved; there is no remedy to be found for my pain. I have become a wanderer [far] from my land. Will you delay me here? . . .

I have become dust on your path; you protect me exceedingly well. Are you those stone-breasted mountains over there, swelling their breasts across from me?

Snowy mountain! Coming down on my road like a robber. I have been separated from my Beloved. Will you bar my way?

Cloud, hanging in clusters on the head of the snowy mountains, will you let down your hair and secretly weep for me?

And, finally, in Poem LXX, in a poem addressed apparently to a human beloved, perhaps female even though the human beloved is usually male, Yūnus uses unconventionally homely similes to describe his loved one:

The purity of your appearance is like bulgur [boiled and pounded wheat] and chick-peas. Your two eyebrows and moon forehead give a lesson to the new moon.

Yūnus's poetry is written so that each line can usually be divided in two by a caesura, with internal rhyme, resulting in a *dörtlük* (quatrain), an ancient Turkish poetical form. Yūnus also uses *redīf*, a word repeated after the rhyming word in each verse, a device that renders the poetry, with its marked beat, even more rhythmically musical.

These elements—the understandable language, the folk meters, and the musical accompaniment—helped make Yūnus's poetry and message so powerful and enduring that it can be recited by heart by most Turks even today. As for his message, it derives from a system of belief that Yūnus shared with other *ṣūfī*s: the belief in the immanence of God in all creation, as well as in the ascending levels of spiritual perfection, beginning with the inanimate and rising to the spiritually elect, the saints, and the prophets of God. The final goal of all is unity with God, whence all came and whither all strive to return. On this journey intellect and reason are of only limited help: only God-inspired love can bring one to unity with God.

YŪNUS'S WORKS

Yūnus's works consist of a *Dīvān* (his collected poetry) and a didactic work called the *Risālat an-Nushiyya* (*Treatise of Advice*), which begins with a treatment of the Four Elements, the creation of Adam, and the story of Intellect and goes on to discuss Man's states and conditions, such as Patience, Spirit, Anger, and Hate. This treatise, while interesting for the study of Yūnus's thinking, is of limited artistic worth. Yūnus's works have two main foci: (1) the Kuran and the fundamentals of Islam and (2) the Mystical Way, which receives the greater emphasis; they have one principal theme, Love. Yūnus says again and again how difficult is the Path, the Way to God, and how many who have tried to travel it have been lost or gone astray on it. The Path, or spiritual, contemplative way, has as its end love of God and return to Him. One who is accepted as worthy of attempting this goal tries, with the help of spiritual masters, to refine his spirit and body so that he may reach his destination. The world with all its enticements must be renounced to travel on the Path and reach the Goal. Yūnus also speaks constantly of the Friend (God) and says he has seen His face. Using the vocabulary of love-wine poetry, he says he has drunk of the wine (of God's love) and will thus remain intoxicated for eternity, an eternal love. Yūnus frequently refers to himself as *'āşıq*, a word meaning "lover" (as does *emre* itself) and also "folk poet" and "minstrel." In Yūnus's signature as a poet, "'Āşıq Yūnus" or "Yūnus Emre," both meanings are combined.

The one constant theme in Yūnus's poetry is Love, that of God for man and, consequently, man for God. The love of which Yūnus sings is all-powerful, occasioning the creation of the world, and is the force behind the continued existence of the world. Yūnus's love, fierce and burning, completely consumes him. In one of his most popular poems (CXCIV) he describes it thus:

> Love for You took me from myself; it is You I need, You. I burn for You both
>   night and day; it is You I need, You. . . .
> If they should kill me and fling my ashes to the sky, my dust would cry there, "It
>   is You I need, You."
> Yūnus Emre is my name; my fire increases day by day. In the two worlds my
>   goal is this: it is You I need, You.

Two figures with whom Yūnus identifies are Majnūn, the lover of Leyla, who is considered the Lover par excellence, and Hallāj, the "martyr to love," executed in Baghdad in 922. In the eyes of Yūnus and other poets before and after him, both of these men gave up their lives for love: Majnūn suffered, seemingly "went mad," and died, all for the love of Leyla. Hallāj, on the other hand, suffered and died, it was believed, for his extreme statement, "I am God, the Truth." He died for love of God. Their total absorption in love in disregard of all else, including mortal danger, made Majnūn and Hallāj Yūnus's favorite models of the true lover of God. Yūnus, like so many others, was enthralled by the idea of martyrdom.

With love of God, as opposed to attachment to earthly things, comes life eternal (Poem VI):

> O lovers, O lovers, love is sect and religion for me. My eyes have seen the face
>   of the Beloved; all mourning is for me celebration.

In Poem XI:

> For us, love is the *imām* [leader of prayers]; the heart is the Congregation. Our
>   *qıble* [direction of Mecca, to which a Muslim turns while worshiping] is the
>   face of the Beloved; our prayer is continuous.

Yūnus declares, in Poem VI, that God is the soul's original home and its final destination:

> Earlier, also, this intellect and soul's original abode was with You. And in the end again, You will be [my] abode. I am going to go to You.
>
> My path leads from You to You; through You my tongue speaks of You. I absolutely cannot comprehend You; I am astonished by this Divine Wisdom.
>
> May I not say "I" to myself, nor "you" to anyone anymore. Let me not say, "This is the slave; that one is the sultan." Let those who hear be astonished.
>
> Ever since he [Yūnus] came into contact with love of the Friend, this world and the next became one and the same. If you ask about Eternity without beginning and Eternity without end, to me they are like yesterday and today.

Again, in Poem CXXXV, he asserts that love is the foundation of the universe:

> What can I tell the lovers that is sweeter than news of love? I will explain it one by one to those who listen with love.
>
> Before when there was no earth or sky, there was the foundation of love. Love is very ancient, eternal; love brought about everything there is.
>
> At the Primal Feast, at the beginning of Time, whoever saw the Beloved's face his soul was in love; ask him for news of love.
>
> No matter what I try to liken love to, it doesn't work. In this world and the next, what can take love's place!
>
> It is entrusted [to you], guard well the news of love! Do not sit just anywhere and speak about love.
>
> This is the rule among the money changers: they do not show the jewels to those who don't know their worth.

Yūnus describes himself as the distracted lover of God. External forms of religion are dismissed as not important; reward and punishment are beneath the proper concern of the true lover of God, who thinks only of Him and of nothing else (Poem XII):

> If you ask about religion and religious community, what need is religion to the lovers? A lover is completely distraught; a distraught person does not know about religion and religiosity.
>
> The eye of the heart of the lovers has gone to the Beloved. What remains of the external form to practice asceticism and worship?
>
> The one who worships is destined for Heaven; he who does not obey the injunctions of religion is for Hell. [The lover] is free of both of these; what does this indicate?
>
> Whoever loves the Beloved must go to the Beloved; being totally occupied with the Beloved, he will be free from all [other] matters.

As a consequence:

There will be no final questioning and reckoning for him who abandons this world [and] the next. Since he has abandoned all desires, how can Münker and Nekīr [the two angels who question the dead about their deeds] question him about anything?

There will be no fear or hope there for the person who has abandoned both wealth [and] poverty. There will not be room there for knowledge or works; there are no scales there or bridge.

Yūnus's use of fresh and simple metaphors in conveying his message is a particularly attractive characteristic of his poetry. In Poem VIII, for example, in stressing thefoolishness of attachment to the world and externals, Yūnus makes charming use of the image of a tall tree:

One day you will pass away; your great height will descend to the ground. Your branches will go into the fire; the cauldron will boil, the iron plate will get hot.

Discussing the impermanence of this world in Poem XVIII, Yūnus describes how all creation is occupied in praising God, the task (*zikrullāh*, litany of praise of God) of the dervish:

O man of love, open your eyes; look at the face of the earth. See how these lovely flowers, bedecking themselves, came [and then] passed on.

These, bedecking themselves in this way, stretching out toward the Beloved—ask them, brother, where they are going.

Every flower, with a thousand coquettish airs, praises God with supplications. These birds with pleasant voices recite litanies to that King.

They praise His power and His being capable (?) of every task. Yes, thinking of the shortness of their lives, their faces pale.

Their color changes; they fall to the ground again. This is a warning to him who understands. The ones skilled in mystical matters will heed this. . . .

You know that he who comes passes on; you know that he who settles down moves on. Whoever is informed of the significance of this drinks the wine of love.

The poet treats this theme again in Poem LXXXV:

Put aside the ornaments of the world; this world is wind and illusion. How will it be faithful to us, for adversity is [waiting] in ambush.

Don't seek transitory life; for whom did the earth remain everlasting? A hundred thousand kings, a hundred thousand sultans, left dominion and wealth, spent in vain.

Many extensions of hope were our traveling companions. Other than thoughts about the Beloved, all are totally worthless.

Yūnus also says that mere learning is no way to achieve knowledge of God and that it can even prove to be a barrier (Poem XXXI):

> Learning itself is a veil to the eye; learning is the reckoning of this world and the other world. *The* book is indeed the Book of Love; what is this [other] page that is read?
>
> Watch out! Open your eyes; perceive the trap of the carnal self. Move on to the station of the Beloved; what better station could there be?
>
> You say: "My eye sees; it distinguishes pretensions from real meaning." During the day the sun gives light; [then] what is this lamp burning at night?

And again (Poem XLI):

> University professors haven't read this lesson. They were so helpless, they did not know what chapter it was.

Yūnus not only praises the glory of God and His love but bewails his own separation from God. Suffering from neglect by God, Yūnus seems to berate Him for unjust treatment in Poem XXXVII:

> You are closer to us than we are [to ourselves], [but] You are not visible. What is this barrier? Since there is no defect on Your beautiful face, what is this veil?
>
> You said, "He shows the way toward what He wants." You have no partner, O King. Who is guilty; what is [this] reproach?
>
> Who is the writer on the Tablet? Who is He who leads astray, and he who strays? Who is the person who regulates these matters? What is the answer to this question?
>
> Your name is Merciful; You told me of Your mercy. What is this discourse which Your spiritual guides give good news of: "Don't cut off hope [of God's mercy]"?
>
> You know these matters; it is You who give them, You who take them away. Since You know whatever I have done, what is this Trumpet and Accounting?

His *münācāt*, or final prayer at the end of the work (Poem CCIII), pursues this theme in a bitter tone:

> I treated myself cruelly; I sinned. What did I do to You, O King?
>
> Before I came, You said my right share was bad; before I was [even] born, You said, "Adam is very rebellious.". . .
>
> Was it I who fashioned me? [No], it was *You* who fashioned me. Why did You create me filled with faults, O One Without Needs!

Then, discussing the Ṣırāṭ bridge, which all must cross in order to get to Heaven:

> Did I eat my daily bread and [thus] leave You hungry? Or did I eat Your meal and leave You in need?

13

You stretch a bridge like a hair, saying, "Pass over. Come, so that you may
    release yourself from My trap."
Can a man pass over a bridge like a hair? Either he'll fall or manage to hang on
    or fly.
Your slaves make a bridge for good [purposes]. The good is so that they may
    pass over [or] for an excursion.

Yūnus believed he existed with God before there was Existence, before the creation
of the world and everything in it. He vividly describes his life with God before Time
(Poem LXXXVIII):

Before coming to this world I was with the Sultan of the World. I was in the
    dominion of that Sultan whose speech is true, whose command is in effect.
Before the created universe came here, before skies were filled with angels,
    before this realm had a foundation, I was with the Creator of the Domain.

And in Poem XCI, he speaks as if he has merged with God, and as if he has become one
with the New Testament and the Kuran:

Tell the lovers, I am the one who gives my heart for love. Being a bird of love,
    I plunge into the seas.
Taking water from the face of the sea, I offer it to the skies. It is I, going about
    like a cloud, who come close to the throne of God.
Becoming lightning, flashing in the skies, I rivet the angels [to their places]. It
    is I who rule the clouds; it is I who become rain and rains.
I saw the angels of the skies; each one was occupied with some task. They
    praise God with litanies. I am both the New Testament and the Kuran.

Then he quite explicitly says (in Poem CIV) that in primordial time he was God, and
God was he:

I was a star for a long time; in the skies the angels were desirous [of me]. The
    all-compelling God commanded; I was There then.
Before I was in this form, when my name wasn't Yūnus, I was He, He was I; I
    was with the one who offered this love. (?)

Yūnus describes death and the dead as if at first hand, as well he might. He lived
in chaotic times and could very well have witnessed Mongol depredations and the
dreadful consequences of tribal and dynastic fighting. His poems on death seem to me
much more forceful than those of other early poets, such as Aḥmed Faqīh, who seemed
to be trying to terrify the people into fearing God. Yūnus's poetry, on the other hand,
seems to be describing events and signs that he witnessed personally and that moved him
so much he had to recite them to others. Death is most vividly, and sometimes
horrifyingly, described, as in Poem CIX:

I don't know at all whose turn it is; Death strolls about among us. He made the people [his] garden; Death plucks whom he wishes.

He ruins many a one; he destroys the property of many. He makes many shed tears; he destroys all their strength.

He takes the sibling of one; he cries a torrent of tears. The wound of his heart will never heal; Death comes without warning.

Death doesn't let a youth live until, growing to maturity, he knows himself. Laughing, leaving one he narrows his eyes, fixing them [upon others].

Where is his beloved Friend? Worship, go purely, wretched Yūnus; how can he endure [when] Death swallows [even] dragons?

And (Poem CXVI):

I strolled about in the morning; I saw the graves. I saw those delicate bodies, mixed with the black earth.

Bodies decayed [within] the earth, hidden inside the grave. I saw the emptied vein[s], flowed blood, shrouds soaked in blood.

I saw the ruined graves, filled up [with earth], all their houses ruined. All helpless from anxiety; what difficult states I saw!

The summer pastures no longer could be used as summer pastures; the winter pastures no longer could be used as winter pastures. I saw in mouth[s] tongues that had become rust-covered, that could no longer speak.

Some [taken by death while occupied] in pleasure and merrymaking, some [occupied] in music and [pleasure of] good news, some in torment; I saw days that had become nights.

Those black eyes had lost their luster; their moon faces had become blurred. Under the black earth I saw hands that arranged roses. . . .

Some moaning, crying, the unfortunate ones burning with suffering [lit. flames brand their souls]. I saw their graves on fire, with smoke coming out.

Reading these poems, it is easy to imagine that Yūnus had personal experience of the destruction and havoc so prevalent in his day.

Another strong theme that runs through Yūnus's poetry is that of disdain for the formal requirements of religion. Yūnus, as a member of the spiritual elect, seems in some poems to consider himself above conforming to mere external practices, established, as he sees them, for those whose faith is weak. As he says in Poem CLXVIII:

Do not say about me, "He doesn't perform his prayers." I know my prayers.
    Whether I perform them or don't perform them, God knows my supplication.
Other than the Beloved, no one knows who is a Muslim and who a misbeliever.

Yūnus also wrote poems (such as Poem XXXIX) in which he stresses the necessity of strict adherence to the religious laws, which, for those who obey, will result in the rewards in Heaven of houris and the wine of the river Kevser. Of all these themes and ideas, however, the most dominant and compelling one is that of love (Poem XCV, not in Fatih manuscript):

> I wander, burning; love dyed me with blood. I am neither rational nor mad; come
>   see what love has done to me.
> Sometimes I blow like the wind; sometimes I raise dust like the roads.
>   Sometimes I flow like the floods; come see what love has done to me.
> I murmur like flowing streams; I brand my pain-laden liver. . . .
> I am wretched, poor Yūnus, covered with wounds from head to toe. I am a
>   wanderer separated from the land of the Beloved; come see what love has
>   done to me.

And (Poem XCIV):

> My soul, I have come from There [beginning of time] to here as an eternal lover.
> Taking love as a guide I started out on the road and came.

YŪNUS'S INFLUENCE

Yūnus is considered the first significant Turkish mystical poet of Anatolia. His influence on successive generations of Anatolian poets was enormous, and a number of "Yūnuses" appeared after him. This makes the problem of determining exactly which poems Yūnus Emre himself wrote an extremely difficult one, of course. His *taṣavvufī* (mystical) poems have been warmly embraced by the dervish orders (*ṭarīqat*s), especially the Kızılbaş and the Bektaşīs, ensuring the preservation of the poems and also their lasting influence upon *tekke* literature.

One can only guess at the actual influence Yūnus may have had upon the Islamization of Anatolia. But since he played such an important role in *tekke* life and, I believe, in the faith of those in the countryside, such as those nomads he traveled with, one can very well imagine his religious influence to have been extremely important. It was, after all, not the *medrese*s and the city-based mosques which converted the countryside, but rather the holy men and traveling sheikhs like Yūnus.

Yūnus's poetry endures. His eternal message of love remains as fresh and vital today as it was in the fourteenth century, and parts of the poems have even become proverbial sayings still in use in modern Turkey. Although the Turks have enthusiastically claimed Yūnus as their own, his audience was originally, and is today, all humanity.

Notes on Translation

I have chosen the Fatih manuscript (F: Istanbul Süleymaniye Kütüphanesi, no. 3889) as the basis of my translations. A photocopy of the manuscript is published in Abdülbâki Gölpınarlı's *Yunus Emre—Risâlat al-Nushiyya ve Dîvân* (Istanbul, 1965). Page, folio, and poem numbers cited in the poems refer to this work. I have also consulted the manuscript Halet Efendi no. 688, the Dil ve Tarih Coğrafya Fakültesi Kütüphanesi (TDTC) manu-script no. 185 (dated 988/1580-81), and the photostat of the Ritter manuscript (R) (MS or. oct. 2575), fourteenth century (?), from the Türkiyat Enstitüsü, to emend the Fatih manuscript text.[1]

I believe this procedure responds better to the challenge posed by the great variety among the texts and manuscripts of the preserved poetry—and to the nature of Yūnus's art—than would a conventional *édition critique*. As I mentioned above, from what is

---

1 Other important manuscripts are the following:
   1. Karaman manuscript. A microfilm of this important manuscript is held in the Milli Kütüphane in Ankara, MFA (D) 12. It contains 211 poems. Dr. Mujgân Cumbur considers it to be an excellent, and possibly the oldest, manuscript, perhaps from the early fourteenth century. I was told, however, that according to the conditions set down by the owner of the manuscript, it is not available for study.
   2. Bursa İl Halk Library manuscript. Eski Eserler Bl., 882, fifteenth century (?), 115 poems.
   3. Nuruosmaniye manuscript. No. 4904, contained in the work *Câmiül-Meânî* (172b-195a), transcribed in 940/1540.
   4. Raif Yelkenci manuscript. Fourteenth or fifteenth century (?), 182 poems.
   5. Yahya Efendi manuscript. Süleymaniye 3480. According to Gölpınarlı, this was transcribed in the sixteenth century. It contains 302 poems.
   For a discussion of these and other manuscripts, see Gölpınarlı, *Yunus Emre—Risâlat al-Nushiyya ve Dîvân*, Önsöz, pp. 49-53. Also see Mustafa Tatçı, *Yunus Emre divanı:* [vol.] *I. İnceleme;* [vol.] *II. Tenkidli Metin;* [vol.] *III. Risaletü'n nushiyye: Tenkitli metin* (Ankara: Kültür Bakanlığı, 1990-91), vol. I, pp. 1-11; and idem, "Yunus Emre'ye ait divanlar, divan neşirleri ve metin tamiri mes'elesi," *Milli Eğitim* 83 (March 1989): 60-71.

now known of Yūnus, his poetry seems to have been of oral, rather than written, composition and was thus revised, recomposed, or re-created by him at every recital. The transmissions of his work, whether through memory or copy, would thus also have varied as they derived from different recitals, producing eventually the enormous differences, indeed discrepancies, that are so evident in the surviving materials.[2] Application of the method of critical editing, which attempts to recover the original text of a written work, to these originally oral materials would be both unproductive, since there is no written original to recover, and meaningless, since there was not one original, but many, potentially one from each recital. Since recovery of *the* original is impossible and presentation of all originals unmanageable, I offer only a good version taken from a sound—and soundly complemented—manuscript.

---

2   "The song is always changing because it is constantly 'a text in the process of becoming' [quote from Paul Zumthor], undergoing mutations through performance, oral transmission, scribal revision and the intentional spinning of new versions" (Joseph Duggan, "Editing Medieval Texts," *University Publishing* 9 [Summer 1980]: 17).

Translations of the Poems

I

p. 38; f. 55b

sensüz yola girürisem çārem yok adım atmaġa

Meter: 8/8

1   If I were to start out without You, I could not take a step. You are the strength
in my body [that allows me] to raise my head and walk.

2   My heart, my soul, my intellect, my knowledge, are firm because of You.
One's wing of the soul must be spread, flying to go to the Beloved.

3   He who passes beyond his Self, the Beloved makes a hawk. He looses him on
the ducks and partridges, driving and reaching them, to catch them.

4   God gave the man of love the strength of a thousand Ḥamzas. He removes
boulders from his way; he intends to go to the Beloved.

5   A hundred thousand Ferhāds, taking their picks, dig away at the base of the
mountains. Breaking up the boulders, he makes a road to let the Water of
Life flow.

6   The fountain of the Water of Life is the union of lovers. Its pleasant
conversation inflames the thirsty ones with His love. (?)

7   Should I call him a lover who loves God's Paradise? Paradise itself is a trap
to catch the souls of the foolish ones.

8   The lover is wretched; he submits to the path of God. Whatever you say, he
accepts; it is impossible to hurt his feelings.

9   We knew that those who came passed on; we saw that those who settled down
passed on. [But] souls who have drunk the wine of love do not accord with
passing or settling.

10   Yūnus's soul was not trapped; it passed beyond Hell and Heaven. He has set
out to go to the Beloved, to sink into His essence.

Halet Efendi, f. 1b; TDTC, ff. 104b, 105a.

4 Ḥamza was an uncle of the Prophet who was famous for his strength. He fell at the battle of Uḥud.

5 Ferhād was a famous lover in Persian literature. He undertook to remove a mountain so that a river could flow in front of his lover Şīrīn's palace.

6 TDTC, f. 105a, has *qadeḥın tolu yüridür susamışlar kandurmağa.*

II

pp. 38, 39; ff. 56b, 57a

ʿışqdan davī kılan kişi hīç aňmaya ḥırṣ u hevā

Meter: 8/8

1   He who makes claims of love will never think of greed or desire. Those who enter the house of love will no longer [have] either affection or faithfulness.

2   Glory and high officials' [offices], all of these [indicate] love of the world. [If they were to ask me, I would say,] "You give my answer: my honor is [the] price [I will give] for love."

3   Those who speak of love with their tongue do not know what love is. Whoever loves the world's glory should not speak of love.

4   Whoever has not gone beyond glory and honor, [to say that he has attained] the state of being a lover is a false accusation. Horses, mules, and camels cannot pass to the lover's bed.

5   Saying "Yūnus is a lover," beware [of imitating him]; do not strive to come [on his path, since] many merchants upon setting out on the long road [later] regret it.

Halet Efendi, ff. 2a, 2b.

III

p. 39, ff. 57a, 57b

bir gün yüzün gören kişi ömrince hiç unutmaya

Meter: 8/8

1   The person who sees Your face one day will not forget it as long as he lives. On his tongue You will be his prayer praising God; he will not say anything else.

2   If the rigid ascetic rises to pray and his eyes should happen to see You, he will forget his prayer beads and will not prostrate himself any more.

3   While taking sugar into his mouth, he whose eyes should happen to fall upon You will forget that sugar and will not chew and swallow it any more.

4   Because I love You, if they were to ask (?) Your price, [I would say] if I were to give the wealth of the two worlds [this and the next], still its worth would be insufficient.

5   If the two worlds were completely filled with vineyards and gardens, a rose with an aroma better than Yours would not grow in [any] garden.

6   The Beloved suffices [as] the aroma of roses and sweet basil for the lovers. The lover's Beloved will never leave his presence.

7   When Isrāfīl blows his trumpet on the Last Day, and when all creatures rise from their graves, my ear will hear nothing besides Your voice.

8   [Even] if Venus were to descend to earth and play her instrument, [since] You are the revelry of the lover, his eye will not go in that direction [toward Venus].

9   What are family and home worth, and the two worlds, without You? No one should doubt that the two worlds are sacrificed for You.

10   If the houris of the eight heavens, adorning themselves, should come, my heart would not accept anything other than Your love.

11   What [good things] can be in this world that will not be in the next world? When the houris and the male servants of Paradise come, the lover ought not to stretch out his hand to them.

12   Ever since Yūnus loved You, glad news has come to his soul. Every moment he is in a new life, he will never use up his life.

Halet Efendi, ff. 2b, 3a.

5   Add *ger* (Halet Efendi, f. 2b).

7   Isrāfīl is the Angel of Death who will blow the last trumpet.

8   The planet Venus is the star of musicians and is also associated with pleasure and sensuality.

9   Reading *sensin* (Halet Efendi, f. 3a) instead of *sensüz*.

10   Adding *göñül* (Halet Efendi, f. 3a).

IV

p. 40; ff. 58a, 58b

iki cihān zindānısa gerek baña bustān ola

Meter: 8/8; 4 müstefʻilün

1   [Even] if the two worlds were a prison, for me they would be a garden. No more worry and grief for me because there will be favor from the Friend.

2   I will go to that Friend, be [His] slave, opening, be a rose. Also, singing I shall be His nightingale; my stopping place will be a rose garden.

3   My eye saw the Beloved's face; my face is dust before the saints. For those who understand speech, my speech will be a field of sugarcane.

4   Every person who gives up worldly claims and flies to the Beloved—the person who has drunk the wine of love—will sometimes be drunk, sometimes intoxicated.

5   Without You the two worlds appear to my eyes as a prison. He who is familiar with Your love, must be the select of the select.

6   My inner self was not satiated with love; involuntarily I speak. Yūnus, this message of yours will be a legend to the two worlds.

Halet Efendi, f. 3b.

4   "Wine," reading *şarābın* (Halet Efendi, f. 3b).

V

'ışq eteġin tutmak gerek 'aqibet zevāl olmaya

Meter: 8/8; 4 müstef'ilün

1   One must cling to the hem of love, so in the end there will not be a passing away. He who reads one *elif* from [the story] of love will not be questioned by anyone.

2   If you hearken to what love says, if you follow it with all your soul, on the road of love the soul is the ransom, not material possessions.

3   If you want to know what the mark of [spiritually] noble men is, [it is:] even if he is just a boy, there will be nothing sinful or hurtful in his speech.

4   The sign of the adepts of spiritual learning is this, it will be present in each one's heart: he will surrender himself [to the will of God], and in his speech there will be no malicious talk.

5   Don't you see the bee; he gets honey from every flower. [But] in the nest of the fly and the moth there will not be any honey.

6   If you wish pearls and jewels, serve the spiritual adepts. If an ignorant person speaks a thousand words, it will not amount to a dram of meaning.

7   Wretched Yūnus! In the hand of love, deadly poison becomes an antidote. Knowledge and works, asceticism and worship—enough of these, without love they will not be canonically lawful.

Halet Efendi, ff. 3b, 4a.

1   Reading *bir* (one) (Halet Efendi, f. 3b); *elif* is the first letter of the alphabet.

6   "Pearls and jewels" refer to clever, beautiful, and/or intelligent words.

VI

p. 41; ff. 59b, 60a, 60b

iy 'āşıqlar, iy 'āşıqlar
mezheb u dīn 'ışqdur baña

Meter: 8/8

1   O lovers, O lovers, love is sect and religion for me. My eyes have seen the face of the Beloved; all mourning is for me celebration.

2   O King, O King! Look, I gave myself to You. You are all my treasure and treasury from beginning to end.

3   Earlier, also, this intellect and soul's original abode was with You. And in the end again, You will be [my] abode. I am going to go to You.

4   My path leads from You to You; through You my tongue speaks of You. I absolutely cannot comprehend You; I am astonished by this Divine Wisdom.

5   May I not say "I" to myself, nor "you" to anyone anymore. Let me not say, "This is the slave; that one is the sultan." Let those who hear be astonished.

6   Ever since he [Yūnus] came into contact with love of the Friend, this world and the next became one and the same. If you ask about Eternity without Beginning and Eternity without End, to me they are like yesterday and today.

7   There will not be any more mourning for us; our hearts will not have rust on them at all, because the voice coming from God is a celebration without end for me.

8   Let me not be separated from Your love; let me not leave Your court. If I go away from myself, together with You I will reach my [true] self.

9   That Friend sent me; "Go, see this world," He said. I came; I saw that it is beautifully adorned, [but] he who loves You will not stay there.

10 He promised His servants; He said, "Tomorrow I will give you Paradise."
My tomorrow, which those friends rejoice in, is today for me.

11 Who is to understand this inner wisdom with this moaning and sighing? Even
if one understands it, it is ineffable. I turned my face to You.

12 You are soul and world for me; You are the secret treasure for me. Profit and
loss are from You; what could [possibly] come *from* me *for* me?

13 Yūnus has turned his face toward You; he has completely forgotten himself.
He speaks entirely to You, [but] it is You who make him speak.

Halet Efendi, ff. 4a, 4b.

6   Reading *dōst 'ışqına ulaşlıdan* (Halet Efendi, f. 4a).

7   "Rust" refers to the traces of material existence which becloud the soul's [heart's]
mirror.

13   Reading *sensin* (Halet Efendi, f. 4b).

VIII

p. 42; ff. 61b, 62a

gideridüm ben yol sıra, yavlak uzamış bir ağac

Meter: 8/8

1   I was going along the road, [I saw] a tree stretched tall. It was so charming, so sweet, my heart said, "Reveal a few secrets!"

2   What sense is it to stretch [so] tall like this? Because this world is transitory. This is the mark of excessiveness; come here, pass over to humbleness.

3   Adorning yourself so charmingly like this, and decorating yourself so sweetly, the heart stretching out to God—What is [your] wish? What do you need?

4   Trees grow old, time passes; the bird alights [just] once on the branch. Birds have not alighted on you yet, neither dove nor francolin.

5   One day you will pass away; your great height will descend to the ground. Your branches will go into the fire; the cauldron will boil; the iron plate will get hot.

6   Yūnus, you have many faults; compared to [the tree], you have a hundred thousand times more. Rather than asking the way of a dry tree, go on your way, diverting yourself.

Halet Efendi, ff. 5a, 5b.

IX

p. 43; ff. 62a, 62b

sen bu cihān mülkini qāfdan qāfa dutdun tut

Meter: 7/7

1   Imagine that you have this world's wealth from the Qāf Mountains to the Qāf Mountains. Or imagine that wagering, you won the possessions of this world.

2   Imagine that you have sat happily on the throne of Solomon. Imagine that you have ruled absolutely over devils and fairies.

3   Imagine that you have added Pharaoh's treasury and the treasury of Nushīn-revān to the wealth of Qārūn, and added [all] that to your wealth.

4   This world is a [mere] morsel; understand that it is chewed in your mouth. Since it is chewed, how can one keep from swallowing it? Look! Imagine you have swallowed it.

5   Your life is like an arrow in a bow which is completely drawn. What can stop the drawn arrow? Imagine you have shot it.

6   Every breath that comes from the purse [of the total supply of breaths] shortens life. Since the purse has split open, imagine you have used it up.

7   Since you have sunk into the sea, the water has come up to your throat; don't struggle like a madman, O helpless one, imagine that you have sunk.

8   Yūnus, even if your life should last a hundred years, [filled] with pleasantness, its final end is a breath. Go beyond that also, and imagine that you have passed through.

Poem IX

Halet Efendi, ff. 5b, 6a.

1   That is, from one end of the world to the other. The Qāf Mountains are the high mountains believed to surround the world.

2   Süleymān is King Solomon.

3   Pharaoh (Firʿawn): In Islam he is the prototype of pride, lust, and attachment to self. Here he is used as a symbol of a possessor of great wealth. Nushīn-revān was a Sassanian king of Iran in the sixth century. Qārūn is mentioned three times in the Kuran (28:76-82, 29:39/38, and 40:25/24). He was known for his great wealth.

XI

p. 44; ff. 63b, 64a

'ışq imām(dur) bize göñül cema'āt

Meter: 6/5

1   For us, love is the *imām*; the heart is the Congregation. Our *qıble* is the face of the Beloved; our prayer is continuous.

2   Upon seeing the Beloved's face, polytheism was taken away. That's why the Holy Law was left at the door.

3   The heart prostrates itself in the *miḥrāb* of the Beloved. It strikes its head upon the ground and supplicates God.

4   There is no "time" like the silent and fervent prayers There [because he has gone beyond times and states]. (?) Whoever is with the Beloved; that moment is *halvet*.

5   The Holy Law says, "Be sure you don't neglect [the stipulations] of the Holy Law." [But] stipulations are for that person who is perfidious.

6   The breath of those who achieved mystical knowledge is a fortunate symbol. With it we became secure from trouble.

7   At that first time in time, we said, "Yes" [when God said, "Am I not Your Lord?"]. It is still one moment, [from] that time [*vaqt*] [to] this hour.

8   Five of us assembled together, [we] arrived at one time; making five one, who will worship. (?)

9   We do not oppose anyone's religion; when religion is complete, love is true.

10   He who guards Truth at the Beloved's door, without doubt will find divine fortune.

11   At that door Yūnus is the lowest of servants; this honor [of service has lasted] from Eternity without Beginning to Eternity without End.

Poem XI

Halet Efendi, ff. 7a, 7b; TDTC, ff. 1331a, 1331b.

1 An *imām* is a leader of prayers. *Qıble* is the direction of prayer; the Kaaba in Mecca.

2 By "polytheism," he is referring to the attribution of a partner to God.

3 The *miḥrāb* is the niche in a mosque indicating the *qıble*. "Head," lit. "face."

4 *Vaqt* "time"; i.e., the moment a mystical state is granted to a *ṣūfī*. *Halvet* refers to retirement from the world for the purpose of devotion.

5 *Xıyānet*, "treachery, ingratitude, perfidy." The idea reappears over and over again in literature that the ungrateful person (to parents, to God, and by extension to His Holy Law) is a terrible wretch.

7 "First time in time": This refers to the Primal Feast, *Ezel Bezmi*; see Glossary.

8 "Five of us": This may refer to the obligatory five daily prayers becoming fused into one continuous act of prayer for the spiritually advanced person.

9 "Love is true": Instead of *toğru* (correct), which Fatih has, Gölpınarlı gives *toğar* (is born) in his transliteration (p. 44) but does not say from which manuscript he has taken his reading. This would result in the reading "Love is born when [one's] religion is complete."

XII

p. 45; ff. 64b, 65a, 65b

dīn u millet sorarısañ, 'āşıqlara dīn ne ḥācet

Meter: 8/8

1   If you ask about religion and religious community, what need is religion to the lovers? A lover is completely distraught; a distraught person does not know about religion and religiosity.

2   The eye of the heart of the lovers has gone to the Beloved. What remains of the external form to practice asceticism and worship?

3   The one who worships is destined for Heaven; he who does not obey the injunctions of religion is for Hell. [The lover] is free of both of these; what does this indicate?

4   Whoever loves the Beloved must go to the Beloved; being totally occupied with the Beloved, he will be free from all [other] matters.

5   Who can bring information about a Beloved such as his? Such was the sign: it could not be contained by the [Angel] Gabriel or the Prophet.

6   There will be no final questioning and reckoning for him who abandons this world [and] the next. Since he has abandoned all desires, how can Münker and Nekīr question him about anything?

7   There will be no fear or hope there for the person who has abandoned both wealth [and] poverty. There will not be room there for knowledge or works; there are no scales there or bridge.

8   In that bazaar of the Last Judgment, every slave will be afraid of losing his head. Yūnus, may you and the lovers never see Doomsday!

Poem XII

Halet Efendi, ff. 8b, 9a.

2   Reading *ma'şuq dapa* (Halet Efendi, f. 8b).

6   Münker and Nekīr are the two angels who will question the dead person about God, His Prophet, His religion, and the Book.

7   "Fear or hope," i.e., the lover will have gone beyond fear of Hell and hope of Paradise. The scales and bridge refer to the scales that will weigh a man's deeds at the time of Resurrection, and to the bridge, Şirāt (non-Kuranic), said to stretch over Hell and over which all must pass. It is thinner than a hair, sharper than a sword. Misbelievers and evildoers will not be able to negotiate this bridge and will fall into Hell.

XIII

p. 46; ff. 65b, 66a

dün gider, gündüz gelür gör nicesi uzgelür

Meter: 7/7

1   Night goes away, day comes, see how many of them come [and go] regularly. By the command of the King, they come straight to the world.

2   Darkness is banished; the world is illumined. The light-lamp [sun] shone; gradually it becomes light.

3   Take a look to the right and left; do not turn off to just any path. Listen to the voice of the birds; [see] how many musical instruments come [to the ear].

4   Look, indeed, the bird itself was the egg, in the nest, on the ground. The voice was the very voice of power; to those who do not know, it seems to be a goose.

5   The Master of Speech takes [back] the speech [when the person dies]; the form remains on the earth. Everyone who knows this state abandons his self.

6   Love took away my "I-ness"; my intellect dispersed to the four directions. Its burden was enough for Yūnus, [but] to one who does not understand, it seemed like a small burden.

Halet Efendi, ff. 7b, 8a; TDTC, f. 78.

4   Reading *xōd yumurdayıdı; . . . O xōd qudret üni* (Halet Efendi, f. 8a).

XIV

p. 46; ff. 66a, 66b

iy beni ayıblayan gel beni 'ışqdan kurtar

Meter: 7/7

1   O one who censures me, come, save me from love. If you are unable to do this, don't speak maliciously.

2   No one proceeds from spiritual state to spiritual state through his own efforts. [It is] the Beloved who determines the states of all of us.

3   Every spiritual state of the lovers comes into existence in the presence of the Beloved. Go! Say [whatever you would] to Him. What [influence] do I have there?

4   Whoever has drunk a swallow from the goblet of love, to him there will be neither stranger nor acquaintance, neither drunkenness nor intoxication.

5   Whoever has removed the veil from the face of the Beloved, no veil remains to him any more, neither good nor evil.

6   I fear to speak because of the punishment of the Holy Law; otherwise, I would have related to you other matters.

7   If Yūnus dies from the sword of the Beloved, there is no reason to grieve, since he who sets in the Beloved's sky rises from the sign of the zodiac of the Beloved.

Halet Efendi, ff. 8a, 8b; TDTC, f. 106.

Note: This poem discusses love, love of God's essence. Every action, word, and state of the one in love with God's essence comes from God because the lover has completely freed himself from everything connected with nonbeing.

Poem XIV

3   Reading *benüm elümde* (TDTC, f. 106, and Halet Efendi, f. 8b).

7   Reading *uyagan* (Halet Efendi, f. 8b).

XVI

p. 47; ff. 67b, 68a

'ışq maqāmı 'ālīdür 'ışq qadīm ezelīdür

Meter: 7/7

1   The station of love is noble; love is very ancient, eternal. He who speaks of love, it is all miraculous speech; his tongue is wholly Power [miraculous Power(?)].

2   It is He who speaks, He who listens, He who sees, He who causes to see. It is He who says every word. Form is the halting place of the soul.

3   How can form find speech, how can it be master of speech? [Rather] it is speech which takes form. Language is the means for divine reason.

4   This is our revelry; it is *that* [love (He?)] which is our delight. What we have drunk and been intoxicated by is the lake of the sherbet-drink of love.

5   Whatever you say is His; it is He who says it; the words are His. He is ours; we are His; this is a different language of praise.

6   [Even] the Unbeliever saw no lie in Yūnus's speech. He who casts his life into darkness is the one deprived of divine knowledge.

Halet Efendi, ff. 9b, 10a.

1   *qadīm*, "very ancient"; i.e., sempiternal, eternally preexistent.
ezelī, "eternal"; i.e., eternal in the past.

XVIII

p. 48; ff. 68b, 69a

iy ʿışq eri aç gözüni yir yüzine eyle naẓar

Meter: 8/8; 4 müstefʿilün

1   O man of love, open your eyes; look at the face of the earth. See how these
lovely flowers, bedecking themselves, came [and then] passed on.

2   These, bedecking themselves in this way, stretching out toward the
Beloved—ask them, brother, where they are going.

3   Every flower, with a thousand coquettish airs, praises God with supplications.
These birds with pleasant voices recite litanies to that King.

4   They praise His power and His being capable (?) of every task. Yet, thinking
of the shortness of their lives, their faces pale.

5   Their color changes; they fall to the ground again. This is a warning to him
who understands. The ones skilled in mystical matters will heed this.

6   Your coming is not [really] coming; your smiling is not [really] smiling. Your
last stopping place is death if you have not experienced [any] trace of love.

7   If you had heard every word, and had washed away this sorrow, if you had
frolicked as you went, this burden of work and care would have left you.

8   You know that he who comes passes on; you know that he who settles down
moves on. Whoever is informed of the significance of this drinks the wine
of love.

9   Yūnus, put aside these words; wash your hands of yourself. Just say what
could come from you since both good and bad come from God.

Halet Efendi, ff. 10b, 11a.

5, 6, 8 *duy*-, "heed" (5); "experienced" (6); "be informed of" (8).

41

XX

p. 49; f. 70b

bu yoklık yolına bugün
bize yoldaş olan kimdür

Meter: 8/8; 4 mefā'īlün

1   Who will be our traveling companion today on this road of annihilation in God? Let's head for our land. Ask! Who will be our brother?

2   Why did we stay in this land, under heavy loads? Who will throw away these burdens and loads and be the sharer of our mystical state?

3   He sent you here. "Walk about and divert yourself, [then] come back," he said. You build buildings, O merchant, but who is the one whose house is dismantled?

4   We saw this face of the earth; we were deceived [by its attractions]. [Yet] we have not been able to reach the Throne of God. O merchant, look! (?) Who is the one who is the Furnisher of this heaven and earth?

5   Come, let's go, for Yūnus has passed on [to the next stage of the journey]; he has started forth. Yūnus prostrates himself. Who is the leader of this road?

Halet Efendi, f. 12a.

2   *yap*, "loads"; or one half of a doublet, synonym for *yük* (load)? *Yap* is apparently a *hapax legomenon*; other guesses at the meaning: "deceits," "wool mats."

5   Reading *gelünüz*, "come," for first word of verse (Halet Efendi, f. 12a).

XXII

p. 50; ff. 71b, 72a

ol 'āşıq cānına kim dōstıla vişāli var

Meter: 8/8

1 Good health to the soul of that lover who has union with the Beloved. His soul is one with his Beloved; what other state could he possibly have?

2 May soul and heart, intellect and understanding, be scattered [like wedding coins] for the sake of his Beloved! For what does the lover have of possessions and property besides [the Beloved]!

3 This land and sky, heaven and earth, are fixed in their places because of the sweetness of love; love is the foundation [of the universe]; [love] always helps the lover.

4 Whoever are lovers must divest themselves of worldly concerns. [The Beloved] commands everything; in every path He has the means.

5 The person who loves eternal life must grasp the hem of love. Other than love, everything changes and declines.

6 For the lovers, this material form is like a shirt. (?) Although a hundred thousand shirts wear out, the lovers [continue to] have endurance.

7 So many people say to Yūnus, "Because you have grown old, abandon love." Time will not touch love; love has no months and years.

Halet Efendi, ff. 12b, 13a.

2 That is, the lover cannot have anything other than the Beloved.

6 "Shirt": The Fatih manuscript has *gökçek*, "shirt." "Endurance," restoring *mecāli*, "their strength, power, vigor."

XXIII

p. 50; ff. 72b, 72b

işidün iy ulu kiçi size benüm xaberüm var

Meter: 8/8

1   Listen, everybody; I have something to tell you. What good fortune I have today, since I have a Beloved such as this.

2   If I walk, You are on my mind; if I speak, You are on my tongue. If I sit, You are beside me. Other than that, what affairs [could I possibly] have?

3   I neither walk, nor even arrive, nor do I set out on long journeys. Since I found the Beloved here, why should I travel any more?

4   Merchants go on long journeys to make a profit, [but] since the jewel is in my hand, say why I should travel any more.

5   Since this soul of wretched Yūnus reached that Beloved, his love increases moment by moment. I have care and attention from a lofty place.

Halet Efendi, ff. 13a, 13b; R, f. 9; TDTC, ff. 160b, 161a.

1   *ulu kiçi*, "everybody"; reading *kiçi* for *kişi* (Halet Efendi, f. 13a; TDTC, f. 161a; R, f. 9, which has a different meter: 7/7).

2   *öğümdesin*, "on/in my mind"; possibly *öñümdesin*, "you are before me."

XXIV

p. 51; ff. 72b, 73a

iy sözlerün aşlın bilen
gel di bu söz kandan gelür

Meter: 8/8

1   O you who know the origin of speech, come, say where this speech comes from. He who does not understand the origin of speech thinks these words come from me.

2   Words turn grief to joy; words make strangers acquaintances. Whether contempt or esteem, it comes to every person through speech.

3   Words are not from black or white, not from writing or reading, not from these people walking around [this animate creation]. They come from the voice of the Creator.

4   I read neither the letter *A* nor *C*; my words are from His Being. A hundred thousand astrologers will not know from which star my fate comes.

5   Light does not come to us from the moon; the man of love is not from this stock. My daily sustenance is not from this house; it comes from the sea of the boundless ocean.

6   We are a pretext there, moreover, say! What can [a mortal] do? [Rather] it is because God commands the soul; the speech comes from Him.

7   Yūnus, moan with pain; what can be at ease in this house of distress? The remedy and atonement for this pain come from a sign and torment.

Halet Efendi, f. 13b.

2   Translating according to Gölpınarlı's note (p. 51) adding *ḳayġuları*, "grief," and *bilişleri*, "acquaintances."

5   "Sustenance": *rızquma* (?), defective spelling.

6   "Pretext": According to a *ḥadīth*, God created the world, and man in it, because He wanted to be known. Thus, man was created for the sake of God, who created all for man.

XXVI

p. 52; ff. 74a, 74b

cānını 'ışq yolına virmeyen 'āşıq mıdur

Meter: 8/8

1   Is he a lover who does not give up his soul for the Path of Love? Is he a lover who does not strive hard to reach that Beloved?

2   Is he a lover who does not, with his [whole] soul, make firm the love of the Beloved in [his] heart? Is he a lover who does not roll up the account book of worldly ambition?

3   One cannot talk about love (?); the ordinary soul does not rise to the skies; he who does not, like a moth, burn in fire, is he a lover?

4   Is he a lover who does not surmount the desires of the carnal self, nor drink from the goblet of love, nor, like a brave man, devote himself to the Path of the Beloved?

5   Is he a lover who does not practice asceticism night and day, kneel during periods of retirement from the world, who does not participate and burn with fervor in the assemblies [of men of mystical knowledge]?

6   Yūnus, now endure the cruelty of that Beloved. Is he a lover who does not set his heart on fire with love?

Halet Efendi, f. 14b.

2   "Account book . . .", i.e., hopes and plans for the future.

6   "Cruelty" refers to God's hiding himself from a devotee.

XXXI

p. 55; ff. 77b, 78a

vuşlati olan kişiye bu derd ile firāq nedür

Meter: 8/8

1   For the person who has achieved union, what is this pain and separation?
    [For] the person who sees the Beloved up close, what is this remoteness he
    looked at?

2   It is necessary for the man who has achieved union that he give up existence.
    This person [who has achieved union], who is going along the road, let's
    see what his provisions are.

3   If you were a man of union, if you understood the veil over the eye, if you
    have seen the Beloved clearly, renounce this existence. What is it [after
    all—nothing]!

4   Learning itself is a veil to the eye; learning is the reckoning of this world and
    the other world. *The* book is indeed the Book of Love; what is this [other]
    page that is read?

5   Watch out! Open your eyes; perceive the trap of the carnal self. Move on to
    the station of the Beloved; what better station could there be?

6   You say: "My eye sees; it distinguishes pretensions from real meaning."
    During the day the sun gives light; [then] what is this lamp burning at
    night?

7   Yūnus is manifest and secret; the two worlds are filled with God. Let him
    who is going to the Beloved come forward; what are houris, palaces [in
    Paradise], and Burāq [to him—nothing]!

Poem XXXI

Halet Efendi, ff. 17a, 17b; TDTC, ff. 90b, 91a.

1   Halet Efendi, f. 17a: *göz ḥıcābın bildünse*; TDTC, f. 91a: *göz ḥıcābın gördüñise*.

7   Burāq is the miraculous steed Muḥammad rode on his Heavenly Ascent (*Mi'rāj*),
     usually pictured as having a human face.

XXXIII

p. 56; ff. 78b, 79a

koyub naqş u nigārı naqşe yol virme zinhār

Meter: 7/7

1 Give up external form and embellishment; be careful! Do not give an opportunity to external form. He who starts out on the way with external form, in the end will love the world.

2 Leave aside the world, worldly goods, and ambitions. This [spiritual] information can definitely not pass through a heart which has two loves in it.

3 Either love the world, hold fast to it, or love the Way and give up [the world] (?). They say that two claims as well as one truth cannot be contained in this road.

4 Give up obedience to created things; do not take your eye away from the presence of the Beloved. Do not be deceived by transitory form; what can they [one] do with transitory form?

5 Do not be stranded at a distance of one hundred thousand years' farsangs, [deceived] by just an ordinary trick. [The spiritual elect] traverse two worlds at one step without becoming confused.

6 Pass through this world of fortune; the caravan has gone; catch up with it. Fear is on the right and on the left. [Those not deceived by external form] go without hesitating.

7 Do not look at the road in the wilderness, [for] the road is at home; do not go outside. The way of the soul is inside the soul; it is the soul which hears the secret of the soul.

8 The soul knows the secret of the soul; the soul will not tell its secret. The true lover speaks with his Beloved in the wilderness.

9   From the first step onward, [Yūnus's, the lover's] true direction is ahead. He came, he goes inside, [but] Yūnus is outside, uninformed.

Halet Efendi, f. 18a; TDTC, ff. 97b, 98a.

5   A farsang is a little over six miles. *değme renk*, "ordinary trick" or "transitory form."

8   *yelen yaban*, doublet, "wilderness, wilderness."

XXXV

p. 57; ff. 80a, 80b

gelün soralum cānlara ṣūretinden noldı gider

Meter: 8/8; 4 müstef'ilün

1   Come, let's ask the souls: What happened to its form, it goes away? After saying night and day, "I am yours," what reason did it find? It goes away.

2   It is not strange if it goes away and leaves its external form. It is not a mistake or lie or slander; [because] word came from the Beloved, it goes.

3   Where are his wealth and possessions? He has left all of them. He took only his good deeds; he is going to the court of that King.

4   He had become such a Beloved that those matters had been arranged. Know certainly that the soul made fun of form and went away.

5   [Form] set up a bargain, and for one piece of money, he broke it again. He became weary of this world; he put on a sleeveless shirt [shroud] and went.

6   A thousand are born; a thousand go; the order came like this. Whoever gets his fill of the world, his goblet is filled; he goes.

7   Morning and night they speak together, saying, "Let's find God." Yūnus says, "The wretched one has found God here"; he goes.

Halet Efendi, ff. 19a, 19b; TDTC, f. 218.

XXXVI

p. 57; ff. 81a, 81b

dervişlik didūkleri bir 'acāyıb durakdur

Meter: 7/7

1   That which they call the dervish state is a curious station. For the person who is a dervish, he must first have existence.

2   When he has attained life, then he should be in unity with God. He must leave aside his wealth and serve spiritual men.

3   Serve those who have arrived at spiritual truth, the one who has looked and seen God; for him who asks for information about You, much abjectness is necessary.

4   God said to the spiritual man, "[You are] Mine." He placed His riches with the spiritual man. The miraculous influence of those who have achieved great spiritual knowledge is a column from earth to the sky.

5   The *muftī*s have not read this title of privilege of the dervishes. How could they know anything about it? This is a secret page.

6   Yūnus, if you are one who possesses mystical knowledge, do not say, "I understood, I know." Take hold of the hem of wretchedness; in the end it is necessary for you.

Halet Efendi, ff. 19b, 20a; TDTC, ff. 177a, 177b.

5   A *muftī* is someone who expounds the Holy Law. *Berāt*, "title of privilege"; official document written in the *dīvānī* script, stamped with the *tuġrā*, stating the name and location of someone being appointed or promoted to a position, his income, and what is expected of him in the way of services.

XXXVII

p. 58; ff. 81b, 82a

sen xōd bize bizden yakın
görünmezsin ḥicāb nedür

Meter: 8/8

1   You are closer to us than we are [to ourselves], [but] You are not visible. What is this barrier? Since there is no defect on Your beautiful face, what is this veil?

2   You said, "He shows the way to what He wants." You have no partner, O King. Who is guilty; what is [this] reproach?

3   Who is the writer on the Tablet? Who is He who leads astray, and he who strays? Who is the person who regulates these matters? What is the answer to this question?

4   Your name is Merciful; You told me of Your mercy. What is this discourse which Your spiritual guides give good news of: "Don't cut off hope [of God's mercy]"?

5   You know these matters; it is You who give them, You who take them away. Since You know whatever I have done, what is this Trumpet and Accounting?

6   Where is the sultan of this realm? If this is the body, where is the soul? This eye wants to see that. What is the refuge of this one who has been taken into God's mercy?

7   Yūnus, this eye won't see that, and those who see won't tell about it. Intellect will not reach this stage. What is this mirage You have left?

Halet Efendi, ff. 42a, 42b.

1   "You are closer to us than we are [to ourselves]" (Kuran 50:16).

2   "He shows the way to what He wants." This appears a number of times in the Kuran (2:142, 213, 272).

3   According to traditional belief, while God was creating the world, He created a large, green tablet and a great pen. God commanded the Pen to write, and it wrote on the Tablet everything that would happen up to the Last Judgment. The original of the Kuran was also inscribed on the Tablet.

5   The Trumpet will sound to announce the Final Reckoning, at which time an Accounting will be made of everyone's good and bad deeds.

XXXIX

p. 59; ff. 83a, 83b

işit sözümi i ġāfil dañla seḥer vaqtinde tur

Meter: 8/8

1   O heedless one, listen to my words; get up early at dawn. The Perfect One [God] has thus commanded: "Get up early in the morning."

2   Listen to what your rooster says: "Your daily portion is given at dawn." Turn your face to the court of the Beloved; get up early in the morning.

3   Listen to my words, O deaf one, so that your scales will be heavy! Beseech God, call upon Him; get up early in the morning.

4   Those lying in bed are in a wretched state. They are incapable of achieving anything. In the morning blows the breeze of mercy; get up early in the morning.

5   Get up with the birds; perform your prayers with the leader of the prayers. Implore God [for mercy because of your] sins; get up early in the morning.

6   Let the Kuran be recited and the thirty-sixth sūra of the Kuran so that you may pay heed and listen. May you wash away your sins, which are like a mountain; get up early in the morning.

7   Let tradition and theology be recited; they say, "Peace be unto [the Prophet]." If you are a lover, let me know it with certainty; get up early in the morning.

8   Paradise will be permitted to you, and you will be permitted to embrace the houris and to drink of the wine of Kevser.

9   Poor Yūnus, open your eyes; rouse yourself from heedlessness. So that you may know yourself, get up early in the morning.

Poem XXXIX

Halet Efendi, f. 43a.

Note: This poem is reminiscent of one of Hoja Aḥmed Yesevī's *hikmet*s (mystical poems), especially the one that begins *Bīdār bolgīl ey mū'mīn seḥer vaqtı*. Aḥmed Yesevī (d. 1166) was an important central Asian poet and founder of a *ṣūfī* order. See Vámbéry, *Čagataische Sprachstudien*, p. 116. The morning prayer is considered to have special virtues.

3   "Scales will be heavy," i.e., so that your good deeds will be heavy when weighed in the scales on the Day of Judgment.

6   The thirty-sixth sūra is often considered the heart of the Kuran. In it are discussed the wisdom of the Kuran, the signs of God in nature, revelation, and the Resurrection and the Hereafter.

8   Kevser is a river in Paradise. For the *ṣūfī*s it symbolizes spiritual knowledge.

XL

p. 59; ff. 83b, 84a

işbu vücūdum şehrine bir giresim gelür

Meter: first line 8/6; then 7/7

1   I want to enter the city of my body right away. I want to see the face of the King who is inside.

2   I hear His words, but I cannot see His face. In order to see His face, I feel like giving my soul.

3   That King's place for retirement and worship has seven cells; I want to stroll about in all of them.

4   At every door there is a person who has one hundred thousand soldiers. I want to gird myself with the sword of love and slaughter them all.

5   The pleasant conversation of the spiritual adepts increases mystical knowledge. I always feel like driving those without grief away from the assembly.

6   I am Majnūn's Leyla; I am madly in love with the Merciful One. In order to see Leyla's face, I feel like becoming Majnūn.

7   The Beloved was [our] guest for many years, a long time. In truth, I feel like being a sacrifice like Ismā'īl.

8   Poor Yūnus's self is inside the four elements. With love I want to secretly reach the secret of the soul.

Halet Efendi, ff. 43b, 44a.

1   "I want to . . . right away," i.e., get behind my material existence.

5   "Those without grief" refers to those lacking spiritual knowledge. Whoever has such knowledge will mourn his separation from God or regret his sins or the transitoriness of existence.

6   Leyla and Majnūn are prototypical lovers and the main characters of a number of works in Turkish and Persian.

7   Ismā'īl was a son of Abraham and was about to be sacrificed when God sent down a sheep to be sacrificed instead.

8   The four elements are fire, air, water, and earth.

XLI

p. 60; ff. 84b, 85a

yandı yüregüm dutuşdı,
baġrum cigerüm kepābdurur

Meter: first line 8/9; then 8/8

1   My heart burned, caught fire. My breast and liver are kebab. The drink of the lovers is the cause of this my pain.

2   Love puts to rights many and love ruins many. Many walk about drunk; whoever is like this is ruined.

3   The Pen wrote with His love; the world is a trifle in respect to love. Among the lovers, even Gabriel is a veil.

4   University professors haven't read this lesson. They were so helpless, they did not know what chapter it was.

5   'Azāzīl made a claim; his claim turned out to be a lie. The punishment for those who make false claims is torture.

6   Those acquainted with love will not die, [nor will] the ones intoxicated in the meeting [of the lovers]. Their concern will always be the harp and lute and *rebāb*.

7   Yūnus, now be wretched, and be a slave to the wretched ones, because God longs for the wretched ones.

Halet Efendi, f. 44b.

3   On the Pen, see Poem XXXVII, note to line 3. *kalem çalınmak*: Gölpınarlı (*Yūnus Emre . . . Dîvân*, p. 225) defines as "to write fate, what will happen (to someone)." The metaphor of Gabriel and the veil stresses the lovers' direct knowledge of God. Even Gabriel, who brought down revelations to Muḥammad, might be considered a veil between them and God.

5   'Azāzīl is the Devil.

6   The *rebāb* is a three-stringed violin. Music is often a part of *ṣūfī* gatherings.

XLIII

p. 61; ff. 86a, 86b

benüm göñlüm gözüm 'ışqdan ṭoludur

Meter: 6/5; mefā'īlün, mefā'īlün, fe'ūlün

1   My heart and eye are filled with love. My tongue speaks of the Beloved; my
    face shines with honor.

2   My body burns like the aloes tree. To the one who sees my smoke, it is the
    breeze of the morning.

3   Coat of mail and breastplates cannot withstand the fire of love. Its arrow
    pierces the soul; it has a strong bow.

4   I call upon my King according to my own tongue. My King says to me
    constantly, "Come!"

5   Will those who love You have reason? [Even] if for a moment they are
    rational, they are *always* mad.

6   Yūnus! Be dust on the path of those who have reached spiritual perfection.
    Their station is higher than the ninth heaven.

Halet Efendi, ff. 45b, 46a.

2   The aloes tree yields a fragrant wood often used for incense.

XLV

p. 62; f. 87b

sensin benüm cānum cānı, sensüz qarārum yok

Meter: 8/8; 4 müstef'ilün

1   You are the soul of my soul; without You I have no stability. If You are not in Paradise, by God! I do not esteem it.

2   If I look, my eyes see You; if I speak, You are my words. Other than observing You, I have nothing I want more.

3   Since I forgot myself, and thus went to You, whatever I say, whatever state I am in, I have no stability even for a moment.

4   If You should kill me seventy times, as they did Jerjis, I would return and go to You because I have no shame.

5   Yūnus, also, is in love with You; show Your face to him. And You are my Beloved; I have no other beloved.

Halet Efendi, f. 46b.

2   "Nothing I want more," lit. "no better prey."

4   Jerjis was a prophet who came after Jesus; he was killed by his tribe seventy times and came back to life seventy times.

XLVIII

p. 63; ff. 89b, 90a

aydıvirem ne kıldugı benümile ol dilpezīr

Meter: 8/7; 4 müstef'ilün

1   I'll tell you what that Beloved has done to me: every moment with new coquetry He makes me a slave again.

2   Wherever I look, it is He who appears before my eyes. I do not have comprehension or discernment suitable [to comprehend] Him.

3   No matter how long I live, freedom [from Him] is impossible for me. The prey caught in the trap is in the hand of the hunter.

4   To the wise, breath is pleasant; do not ask about its characteristics. How can I explain His characteristics? He has no parallel; He is without match.

5   He promised everyone that tomorrow they would see Him. My tomorrow is today; the Almighty appeared here.

6   Yūnus's total gazing is immersed in the face of the Beloved. No place is left where He is not present; every place appears filled with Him.

Halet Efendi, f. 48b; TDTC, ff. 73b, 74a.

LII

p. 66; ff. 92a, 92b

'ışq erinuñ göñli toli pādişāhdan nevāledür

Meter: 8/8

1   The heart of the man of love is filled, it is [his] portion from the King. How can the man without love understand, since the Holy Law is a barrier [to him]?

2   The soul of the lover is love; his home and family are sacrificed for love. The gift of the man of love is an affliction to the person without love.

3   Some love wife and son; some possessions and home; some wealth and shops: this world changes from state to state.

4   What is the lover to do with this world? In the end he will leave it one day. Having taken hold of the skirt of love, he goes; whoever comes [to separate him from this road], he will leave aside. (?)

5   In eternity that King offered me a goblet. Ever since I drank from it, I sigh. I don't know what kind of wine it is.

6   O wretched Yūnus, your distinctive characteristic is [this]: this soul of yours was intoxicated by love. In His court, always be distracted and amazed!

Halet Efendi, ff. 49b, 50a.

1   *ḥavāle*, "barrier." See Şemseddīn Sāmī, *Qāmūs-i Türkī* (Istanbul: İqdām, 1901).

3   "Wife and son" or "women and boys."

4   "This," reading *bu* (in Halet Efendi, f. 50a).

LV

p. 67; ff. 94a, 94b

bize dīdār gerek, dünye gerekmez

Meter: 6/5; mefā'īlün, mefā'īlün, fe'ūlün

1   For us the Face is necessary; the world is not [necessary]. For us the spiritual realm is necessary, not false claims.

2   For us this night is the Night of Power; let it not be morning; dawn is not necessary.

3   O mad one, offer us some of the drink of love. For us [the river] Kevser in Paradise is not necessary.

4   Let us drink bowl upon bowl; completely filled. We won't become drunk; we will not [suffer] stupefaction.

5   Yūnus, becoming drunk, fell into the wooden [drinking] bowl. He calls upon Tapduk; shame is not necessary.

Halet Efendi, f. 51b.

2   The Night of Power was the night when the Kuran was revealed, the twenty-seventh of the month of Ramażān. It is considered the holiest night of the year, when Muslims may spend all night in prayer. The verse does not divide neatly into 6/5.

5   Tapduk was Yūnus's *mürşid*, or spiritual mentor. *Tapdugına* can also be construed here as "the one he worships."

LXVII

p. 73; ff. 102a, 102b

şükür ḥaqqa kim dōst bize
ayıtdı dōst yüzine bak

Meter: 8/8

1   Thanks be to God, for the Beloved said, "Look at the face of the Beloved." I opened my heart's eye and saw my Sultan certainly.

2   Because I saw my God, I became acquainted with God. Wherever I looked, everything seen was all God.

3   The door of God's bridal chamber (?) is open for His friends. If you want to be His friend, read a lesson from the friends.

4   You are veiled today [from God]; they will not show you clearly to yourself. That which I call "veil," understand that I mean "things of the world"; do not esteem them.

5   As long as you are unable to know yourself, and do not regard the spiritual man with favor (?), if you do not put aside your "you-ness," there will be a trap [for you].

6   Seven seas and four rivers will not make you pure. For if your affairs with God did not arrive at a positive result, you remained at a distance [from God].

7   The saints are the door to God; Yūnus is the doorkeeper. He came to this Way with love, and he acquired love also [as] (?) a spiritual station.

3   *duvacuk kapusı* is probably related to *duvak gecesi* (see in the *Derleme Sözlüğü* "*duvak günü*"). The translation "the door of God's bridal chamber" is consistent with the ever-present theme of "union with God." "The friends [of God]" are the saints.

4   Gölpınarlı (*Yunus Emre . . . Dîvân*) adds "*bu*"; without it, the meter is short.

5   "You . . . do not regard the spiritual man with favor": Fatiḥ has *eren naẓar kılmayınca.* "There will be," lit. "was."

LXVIII

p. 74; ff. 102b, 103a

iy çok kitāplar okuyan
sen kim tutarsın baña daḳ

Meter: 8/8

1   O you who read a lot of books, you who find fault with me—so that you will clearly understand the secret, come read a lesson from love.

2   If you knew yourself, if you had left external form, if you knew what "attribute" was, as far as I am concerned, you would have a right to do whatever you do.

3   So that you might not experience bad name and reputation, so that the select and the common people will be as one before you, if you knew knowledge completely, come, come, read a lesson from love.

4   Don't study the exterior of knowledge; deeds are distinguished above knowledge. Open the inner eye of the heart; look at the condition of the lover and the Beloved.

5   Look [at the] lover; see what he is engaged in; he is in that state of excitement toward the Beloved. Both of them are in a complicated state. Looking from afar, don't think that they are two separate [entities].

6   You have not been able to pass beyond duality; you could not differentiate one mystical state from [mere] words. You could not fly to the Beloved. Being a learned man became a trap for you.

7   The robe worn by judges and professors, the dervish cloak, the throne, and the crown must be given as tax for love. 'Abdurrezzāq left four hundred disciples and fifty pilgrims.

8   A great religious personage like him kissed the cross and played the [church] bells. You also, give up your honor, come and burn your idol.

9   One should know that lover and Beloved are one. Every word comes to the tongue from love. Poor Yūnus, how should he know! He read neither black nor white!

2   The Islamic belief reflected here is "He who knows himself knows his lord." "Attribute" (*ṣifat*) is a philosophical concept that has occasioned much discussion. The various religious and philosophical schools held different positions on "attribute." According to the *ṣūfī*s, all attributes are attributes of God; one should not separate the essence or substance from the attribute.

4   *güzīn*, spelled *gūzin* in Fatih.

7   'Abdurrezzāq (also known as Sheikh-i San'ān) was a sheikh who saw himself in a dream worshipping an idol. To understand his dream, he started on a journey with four hundred disciples. When they reached Anatolia, he fell in love with a Christian woman. He put on the Christian girdle, one of the symbols used for Christians, and at the suggestion of the woman, worshipped idols. The sheikh's disciples, having had no success in getting the sheikh to give up the woman and these abhorrent practices, went on the Pilgrimage. At Mecca they prayed for the sheikh, along with another dervish. This dervish saw Muḥammad in a dream and learned that the sheikh had become Muslim again. The woman also had a dream. She followed the sheikh and his disciples and, upon reaching them, became Muslim and died.

8   The sound of church bells is traditionally spoken of as abhorrent to Muslims.

9   "Neither black nor white" refers to black writing on white paper.

LXX

p. 75; ff. 104a, 104b

kerem it bir beri bak niqāb[ı] yüzüñden bırak

Meter: 7/7

1   Be kind; look here; leave off the veil from your face. Are you the moon of the fourteenth day? [Your] face and cheek flash and glitter.

2   Let words from your mouth be permitted, with a hundred thousand thanks, so that tongue and lip might speak out.

3   Like thirty-two pearls arranged on coral, its value is that of pearls; that is appropriate since it is whiter than pearls.

4   The purity of your appearance is like bulgur and chick-peas. Your two eyebrows and moon forehead give a lesson to the new moon.

5   How could he who sees you not fall into the flame like a moth? The glance of your eyes—two candles—takes away the soul.

6   From the sweet murmurings of love, the lover has a chain around his neck. [The lovers] do not want freedom; thus they stayed captive.

7   Which of your attributes can the tongue describe? My God! Hide far from the evil eyes.

8   I was unable to see any difference between your neck and that of a deer. (?) [The only things] that made me doubtful [that your neck was that of a deer] were [your] two earringed ears.

9   Yūnus saw God's manifestation in your face; [therefore] there is no possibility of separation [from you] because God appeared in you.

TDTC, f. 96.

Note: Gölpınarlı thinks this poem important because it is addressed to a young woman with whom Yūnus is spiritually in love. He thinks that perhaps the folk legends that say this poem was written for Tapduk's daughter are true.

1   Translation from TDTC, f. 96. Fatih has *niqābı*, "veil," which results in an extra syllable. The "moon of the fourteenth day" is the full moon and represents the ideal shape of a beautiful face.

3   Fatih has *mirvārī* for "pearl(s)." The correct spelling is *mirvārīd*.

4   Much is made by literary critics of Yūnus's use of such simple things as bulgur (boiled and pounded wheat) and chick-peas in describing his beloved's beauty. "Give a lesson. . .": They are so perfect in form that the new moon even, whose shape is their model, must take a lesson from them. This is an example of the rhetorical figure called disadvantageous confrontation, or etiology, which was much favored by the classical poets especially.

6   "Chain around his neck" refers to the customary method of restraining prisoners.

8   Faruk K. Timurtaş (*Yūnus Emre Divanı*, p. 238) gives the meaning "deer" for *yuvuk*.

LXXII

p. 76; ff. 106b, 107a

ger uluya irdünise şūret naqşi neñdür senün?

Meter: 8/8

1   If you have reached greatness, what is this [material] form to you [why do you still exhibit materiality]? If you have found a path to the spiritual realm, what is this world to you?

2   Give up this world; come and enter the fire of love. Reach the stage ahead; what is this remaining behind of yours?

3   This body's property is not [just] fire and water and earth. Each one of these returns to its source; what is this heedlessness of yours?

4   Idol-temple and wine shop become a mosque to the true soul. Not one coin of yours will be wasted; what is this lying to you?

5   Since you are strong enough [to go] to the Hereafter, leave aside the false pretension [of this world]. If you are a lover [of God], what is this love of goods and treasures to you?

6   If you gather [goods] saying, "They are mine," do you have pretensions of being God? The King will not look at your crime; what is this being lost on the way to you?

7   Night and day you suffer worries; "What should I do? I am a miserable wretch," you say. He is generous; He gives you your daily bread; what is this worry to you?

8   Unfortunate one, eat, feed others; if [food] is lacking, God will provide. One day your body will enter the earth; that which is left behind—what is it to you?

9   Yūnus, you have become very drunk from this goblet of love. While you lost consciousness of self, you reached God; what is sobriety to you?

LXXV

p. 78; ff. 214a, 214b

ne söz keleci dirisem, dilüm seni söyleyecek

Meter: 8/8

1   Whatever words I should speak, my tongue will speak of You. Let me walk wherever I walk; my desire will flee to You.

2   It is true if I should call those who do not love You "lifeless form." That is why someone like You is necessary as a Beloved for those with souls.

3   You said to the whole world You are still within the veil. If You were to walk one moment without a veil, the two worlds would be ruined.

4   Devils and fairies, men and angels, every creature loves You. Before You, houris and angels stand amazed (?).

5   If I should drink fatal poison by Your hand, it would be a wholesome drink. I do not know what spiritual meaning it has, [but] it would become an antidote to my soul.

6   If I were to eat honey and sugar, without You it would be poison to my soul. Since You are the savor of my soul, where could I find one better than You?

7   If a hundred thousand torments should torture my form, my happiness would not decrease at all, [since] to love You would wash all [torments] away.

8   What difference does it make if Mountain Yūnus is a mere particle in love? The earth, sky, and heaven are lasting because of the savor of love.

1   *Hadīth-i qudsī* is sacred, or holy, tradition, any class of tradition that reveals words spoken by God, as distinguished from the *hadīth nabawī*, which transmits the words of the Prophet.

4   *durmuş mıdur* is probably incorrect. I have emended it to *durmuşdurur*, as in an anonymous text in *Tanıklarıyle Tarama Sözlüğü* (Ankara: Türk Tarih Kurumu Basımevi, 1957): houris and angels remain standing before Him in amazement.

LXXXI

pp. 81, 82; ff. 113b, 114a, 114b, 115a

ata belinden bir zamān anasına düşti göñül

Meter: 8/8

1   From out of my father's loins my heart was transferred to [my] mother.
    Permission came from God; my heart went into the treasury. (?)

2   There He made me soul; flesh, bone, and blood He made. In forty days the
    heart began to stir.

3   I walked there secretly; God's command gives no respite. They separated me
    from my homeland; my heart fell to this world.

4   They put me into a cradle, wrapped my hand and leg. From the beginning
    they gave me its pain—my heart fell into salt.

5   Twice a day they loosed [my swaddling clothes]. They arranged silver coins
    around [my] head; they gave me a nipple; my heart fell into the grasp of
    the carnal self.

6   I left behind this [cradle]. I set out to walk. They [almost] opened the twelve
    [rib] bones [when they passed me from one person to another]. The heart
    went from hand to hand.

7   While a boy, he becomes a sultan—some kiss his hand, some his face.
    Intellect became my traveling companion; my heart fell to the role of
    sultan.

8   At this age, my beard grows; those who see it smile. It is found in the
    presence of beauties; my heart became entranced with love.

9   It loves evil more than good; it hurries to do [evil]. It gives rein to the wishes
    of its carnal self; it fell into the house of the carnal self.

10   In its fortieth year, [my] appearance changes: white falls on [my] beard. Seeing the white, my heart fell to pulling it out.

11   It cannot proceed; it cannot achieve youth. Abandoning these, my heart fell to finding consolation.

12   His son says, "He's senile, he doesn't die"; his daughter says, "He doesn't stir." He doesn't know his own state; my heart has gone from one condition to another.

13   When he dies, they will give thanks; they carry him to the grave. They will recite God's name; the heart gave many thanks.

14   They will bring water to wash [the corpse]; they will wrap the shroud [around it preparatory to] placing [it in the coffin]. They will mount it on the wooden horse; my heart fell to the bench of the corpse-washer.

15   If you have [performed] good works, your grave will be wide. If not, your heart has drunk wine of fire.

16   Yūnus, understand your state: your road will come to this; while you can manage this, your heart fell to doing good works.

Halet Efendi, ff. 58a, 58b.

Note: This is similar to a poem by Aḥmed Yesevī (see note to Poem XXXIX), although Yūnus's poem is more autobiographical in nature. See Vámbéry, *Čagataische Sprachstudien*, pp. 117-23.

1   "Treasury," of souls, presumably.

3   "Homeland," of all souls, i.e., God.

5   The text has *başına*, third person singular, "his head."

7   "My heart fell . . . ," i.e., he enjoyed it.

8   *gülregi dutar*, "smile" (?).

14   The "wooden horse" is the corpse-washer's bench.

15   "Wide," i.e., comfortable.

LXXXIV

p. 83; ff. 116a, 116b

dervişlik maqāmı ḥāl içinde ḥāl

Meter: generally 6/5; sometimes 7/6, 7/5, 6/6

1   The state of being a dervish, is one of states within states. For the dervish, the state of unconcern is impossible.

2   The dervish will not be separated from the First Moment; there was no separation [from God], [his] lot is the Lover's Union.

3   Here [in this world] the dervishes have broken the vessel of rebellion [the world?]. They were active; they were not idle. (?)

4   Dervish existence is on the bridge. They have made [their] reckoning [depend upon] a particle of a *miskāl*.

5   If a dervish says, "I am God," what of it? All existence is God's, in every case.

6   Dervish, take not your eye away from the First Moment. Yūnus sees both the End and the Beginning.

Halet Efendi, ff. 60a, 60b.

1   *ḥāl*, "state."

3   Reading taken from Halet Efendi, f. 60a, *uşatdı*, "[they] broke, smashed."

4   Bridge: See note to line 7, Poem XII. *miskāl zerre*, "a mote's weight"; refers to Kuran 4:40; 10:61; 34:3, 22; 99:7, 8.

LXXXV

p. 84; ff. 116b, 117a

koġıl dünye bezeğini bu dünye yildür ye xayāl

Meter: 8/8

1   Put aside the ornaments of the world; this world is wind and illusion. How will it be faithful to us, for adversity is [waiting] in ambush?

2   Don't seek transitory life; for whom did the earth remain everlasting? A hundred thousand kings, a hundred thousand sultans, left dominion and wealth, spent in vain.

3   Many extensions of hope were our traveling companions. Other than thoughts about the Beloved, all are totally worthless.

4   Take into your own hands accounting of yourself. Otherwise, in the hands of the watchmen [on the Ṣırāṭ bridge over Hell] [your] state will be very bad.

5   Kill [the demands] of the carnal self; take it to the bench used for washing the corpse. Otherwise, when [you] die, willy-nilly the washer of the dead will carry you off, dragging [you].

6   Whoever asks you, "What is your belief in God?" kiss his hand and foot; this is the question to his answer. (?)

7   Yūnus, this Straight Road [Islam] is a sacred duty for you. In your presence, at the Resurrection and assembling for justice, union with the Beloved will "be certain truth."

Halet Efendi, ff. 60b, 61a; TDTC, ff. 83a, 83b.

3   *ṭūl al-amal*, "extension of hope," i.e., plans and hopes for the future and worldly ambition. To have such thoughts about the future was considered by *ṣūfī*s to renounce a perfect trust in God.

5   TDTC, f. 83b: *yoḥsa ki keñsüz ölicek süriben iledür ġassāl*

7   "Be certain truth" is a quotation from the Kuran.

LXXXVIII

p. 85; ff. 119a, 119b

bu cihāna gelmedin sulṭān-i cihāndayıdum

Meter: first line 7/8; then 8/8

1   Before coming to this world, I was with the Sultan of the World. I was in the dominion of that Sultan whose speech is true, whose command is in effect.

2   Before the created universe came here, before skies were filled with angels, before this realm had a foundation, I was with the Creator of the Domain.

3   A hundred thousand, twenty-four thousand, of His select four hundred and forty-four levels. In the place of good fortune that day, I was in a noble family [of the prophets and spiritually elect].

4   Pain did not afflict me; worry did not affect me. I was in a lofty place, outside the City of Anxiety.

5   Yūnus, this total existence of yours is not a mite in the presence of the Beloved. I was with the Speech and Word both Here and There.

3   "His select," misspelled *haṣı*.

XC

nite kim ben beni buldum,
yaḳīn bil kim Ḥaqqı buldum

Meter: 8/8

1   Just as I found myself, know with certainty that I found God. Before I found God, [He was] my fear; now I am rescued from fear.

2   I am not afraid of anyone; I don't worry a single bit. Now of whom should I be afraid? I have become close friends with that which I was afraid of.

3   'Azrā'īl won't come to my soul; the Questioner[s] won't come to my grave. What should they ask of me [since] I have become the one who causes the [questions] to be asked?

4   How can I become like Him and command what He commanded previously? He came; our hearts are filled; I became a mine for Him.

5   Those with love take from us; those without love, what can they know? Some take; some give; I became a large shop.

6   God opened the door to Yūnus; Yūnus worshipped God. Eternal glory is apparently mine; [although previously] a slave, I became a sultan.

R, f. 42.

1   This refers to the *hadīth* that "He who knows himself knows his Lord."

2   Reading from the Ritter version (f. 42): *ben kimesneden korkmazam ya bir zerre kayırmazam.*

3   'Azrā'īl is the Angel of Death. The Questioner[s] are Münker and Nekīr; see Poem XII, note to line 6.

4   Meter defective.

XCI

p. 87; ff. 121a, 121b

xaber eyleñ 'aşıqlara 'ışqa göñül viren benem

Meter: 8/8

1   Tell the lovers, I am the one who gives my heart for love. Being a bird of love, I plunge into the seas.

2   Taking water from the face of the sea, I offer it to the skies. It is I, going about like a cloud, who comes close to the throne of God.

3   Becoming lightning, flashing in the skies, I rivet the angels [to their places]. It is I who rule the clouds; it is I who become rain and rains.

4   I saw the angels of the skies; each one was occupied with some task. They praise God with litanies. I am both the New Testament and the Kuran.

5   I understood that the one who speaks [of God] is not the one who sees [Him]; I realized that those who spoke of Him did not know Him. [Rather] it is He who knows; it is He who shows [one the way, the Face]; I am a captive of love.

6   Let it be known that the eight heavens are for lovers, kiosk and *saray* for [the learned]. But it is *I* remaining on Mount Sinai, astonished like Moses.

7   When the Pen writes, see; know that the information is thus: The words ["Am I not your Lord who cherishes and sustains you?"] They said: "Yea!" It is I who inform one here of these things.

8   I have become mad; my name is Yūnus; love has become my guide. It is I who approach His presence alone, prostrating myself.

Halet Efendi, ff. 63b, 64a.

1   *baḥrī*, "kingfisher, sea bird"; could also mean "mariner, sailor."

6   *saray*, "palace."

7   Kuran 7:172 relates how God called forth the as-yet uncreated progeny of Adam and asked them, "Am I not your Lord?" (*alastu bi-rabbikum*). They responded, "Yes, we witness it" (*balā shahidnā*). The echo of this oath of loyalty impels the soul to search for the Truth.

XCII

p. 87; ff. 122a, 122b

ne dirisem ḥükmüm yürür,
elimde fermān dutaram

Meter: 8/8; 4 müstef'ilün

1   Whatever I say, my command is obeyed; I hold an imperial edict in my hand.
    Whatever I do, my command prevails since I hold the command of the
    Sultan.

2   Man and these jinns and fairies and devils are under my command. The wind
    carries my throne; I hold the seal of Solomon.

3   İblīs and Adam, whoever it is, either he [who] goes astray or he [who] leads
    astray—all are mine, good and bad. I control them all because of this
    [imperial edict].

4   The world is my allotted share; its people are my people. Each moment my
    law decision is in effect; I hold my law decision from the Han.

5   While there is a soul like You, I consider him an animal who looks for the
    Fountain of Life and one who enters the darkness.

6   Without Him I would die, I am alive because of Him. Don't believe I always
    cling to life with my soul [with all my power].

7   He is my religion and faith; if I were without Him in the world, I would
    worship neither idols nor the cross. I would adhere to neither religion nor
    faith.

8   Yūnus says: "I am He; do not think me insignificant; I am He. Whatever I
    say, that Beloved obeys, and I obey whatever that Beloved says."

Halet Efendi, ff. 64b, 65a; TDTC, ff. 169b, 170a.

3   İblīs is the Devil, or Satan, who led Adam and Eve astray, with the result that they were banished from the Garden. "Because of this," reading *bundan*. MS unclear, may be *benden*, "because of me."

4   This refers to Kuran 49:13. The idea being stressed is that there is no tribe or nation in Islam. *Yargum urur*: According to Timurtaş, equivalent to *yargum yurur* (*Yunus Emre Divanı*, p. 234).

5   "The Fountain of Life": The allusion here is to the fact that the Fountain of Life was thought to be in a dark place. The person who enters darkness is the one who does not follow God's path but instead tries to attain eternal life.

XCIV

p. 88; ff. 123b, 124a

cānum ben andan [bunda] ezelī 'āsıq geldüm

Meter: 7/7

1   My soul, I have come from There [beginning of time] to here as an eternal lover. Taking love as a guide I started out on the road and came.

2   I do not gossip maliciously, nor am I of the seventy-two languages. There are no strangers to me in this land, having gotten acquainted There, I came.

3   I passed beyond the stage of "I-ness"; I renounced everything. From that gate of duality I came to be [re]joined with [the] Unity, I came.

4   Four people are my traveling companions, faithful and sharers of my secrets. I like three of them, and I became angry with one of them, and I came.

5   One of those four is Soul; one is Religion; one is Faith. One of them is my carnal self, the enemy; fighting with it on the way, I came.

6   They took great pains; they showed us the way. They sent me to this realm; I started out on that road and came.

7   I drank from the wine of love; I passed over eighteen rivers. I pierced the bonds of the seas, overflowing from the ocean, I came.

8   I came here from There, and I will again go There. Knowing that I was going to go There again, becoming acquainted There, I came.

9   What kind of person is 'Azrā'īl that he should have designs on my soul, since I have already settled my accounts with the master of faithfulness, and I came.

10 What matter is it now for Yūnus [to be called] Lover, to be reproached, or to have bad repute? I changed my unbelief to belief There, and came.

Halet Efendi, f. 66; R, f. 88; TDTC, f. 80b.

1   Adding *bunda*, "here," from Halet Efendi.

2   "Seventy-two languages": This road will not be won by words and meaningless pretensions. Although there are seventy-two languages in the world, all have the same meaning. See Kuran 23:51–92, which states that the brotherhood of Truth is one.

6   Adding *bize*, "to us," from Halet Efendi.

7   "Eighteen rivers" refers to the eighteen worlds that compose the universe according to ancient belief. These include Universal Reason, Universal Soul, the nine heavens, the four elements (air, fire, water, earth), and the three kingdoms (animal, vegetable, mineral).

9   'Azrā'īl is the Angel of Death.

XCV

p. 89; ff. 124b, 125a, 125b

sensin kerīm, sensin raḥīm

Allāh saña sundum elüm

Meter: 8/8

1   You are gracious; You are merciful, God; I stretched out my hand to You, God [in supplication]. Other than You, I have no remedy. I stretched out my hand to You, God.

2   The appointed time [of death] has come; the fixed term of life is up; this goblet of my life has filled up. Who remains [alive] without having drunk of it? I stretched out my hand to You, God.

3   My eyes slipped away to the sky; my soul was broken away from my breast; my power of speech is lost. I stretched out my hand to You, God.

4   Look, [my] shroud has been cut out. I have directed my course toward You, God. I wonder what my condition will be. I stretched out my hand to You, God.

5   They washed me; the water [they washed me with] warmed up. My people and siblings all came. Farewell, my people. I stretched out my hand to You, God.

6   My bier came; it is surrounded [by people]; to four sides the call to [a funeral] service is given. The people assemble for prayers for me. I stretched out my hand to You, God.

7   They carried off my bier; they brought it to my grave; they formed a circle and sat down. I stretched out my hand to You, God.

8   When they loosed the corpse [from the coffin]; they sprinkled earth on me. Leaving, they all fled.

9   Seven Hells, eight Heavens, each one has a road [leading to it]. On every road there are one hundred shops. I stretched out my hand to You, God.

10   Münker and Nekīr came; each one questions [me]; they each asked different questions. My God, *You* answer [in my place]. I stretched out my hand to You, God.

11   Look, the times have become strange; cry from [your] heart, since he who is born from a mother dies. I stretched out my hand to You, God.

12   Yūnus, discuss these subjects until it is enough; turn [your] face to your God. Do not separate us from the Face! I stretched out my hand to You, God.

Halet Efendi, ff. 66a, 66b, 67a.

12   "The Face": The vision of the Divine Beloved in Paradise.

XCVI

p. 90; ff. 125b, 126a

benüm bunda qarārum yok,
ben bunda gitmege geldüm

Meter: 8/8

1   I have no permanency here, [since] I came here in order to go away [again]. I am a merchant; I have much merchandise; I came to sell to him who buys.

2   I did not come to [make] pretentious claims; my occupation is with love. The Beloved's abode is the hearts [of men]; I came here to love mankind.

3   My madness is that of Beloved-Intoxication; the lovers know what state [I'm in]. Changing my duality, I came here to be [re]joined with Unity.

4   He is my master; I am His slave; I am the nightingale of the Beloved's garden. Happily I came to that master of mine's garden to sing.

5   Souls that are friends here become acquainted There. Becoming acquainted with my master, I came here to explain my state.

6   Yūnus Emre has become a lover it is said; he has died of the pain of the Beloved. I came to tell of my state at the door of the truly spiritual man.

Halet Efendi, f. 67.

2   "To love mankind" or "to conciliate," *gönüller yap-*.

XCIX

pp. 91, 92; ff. 127b, 128a

ḥaq çalabum, ḥaq çalabum
sencileyin yok çalabum

Meter: 8/8

1   O my God, O my God, there is no one like You! O my very merciful God, forgive us our sins!

2   The slaves belong to You; You belong to the slaves—their sins are many. Place them in Your heaven; let them mount Burāq.

3   You are not [to be found] with sultans or the wealthy, nor in pavilions nor in palaces. You entered the heart of the poor [and] made it Your stopping place.

4   I have neither knowledge nor worship nor strength nor endurance. But I have grace from You; may it make my face white, my God!

5   Pardon Yūnus, along with Your sinful servants. If You do not pardon him, the pains of separation [will be] very great, my God.

Halet Efendi, f. 68b; R, f. 38.

2   Burāq is the winged beast that carried Muḥammad on his Heavenly Ascent.

3   "You entered the heart of the poor" alludes to the *ḥadīth-i qudsī* "Heaven and earth contain me not, but the heart of My Servant does encompass me."

4   "White," i.e., honorable.

C

p. 92; ff. 128a, 128b, 129a, 129b

benüm cānum uyanıkdur,
dōst yüzine bakan benem

Meter: 8/8

1   My soul is awake; it is I who am looking at the face of the Beloved. Also, it
    is I who, in order to mix with the sea, become a river, flowing.

2   Like a river, I'll splash; sometimes I will laugh; sometimes I will cry. I cut
    the liver of the carnal self into small pieces; it is I who destroy (?) pride
    and hate.

3   I destroyed the army of this carnal self; I leveled its towers and ramparts. I
    made its interior pure; it is I who am the purifier of its possessions.

4   I turned my face toward the presence of God; that man of love opened my
    eyes. He showed me to myself; I am the one called the Microcosm of the
    Whole.

5   I saw the King's Face clearly, without doubt, definite, distinct. He who does
    not believe [this] is a misbeliever; it is I who am looking at that Face.

6   All these matters are of my arranging; with my mystical knowledge [I order]
    summer and winter. I know stranger and friend; I am the enduring one
    who does not go away.

7   It is I who am palpitating in all these souls, the one boiling in their veins. It
    is I who speak in all languages, all tongues.

8   It is I who made Nimrūd's fire into a vineyard and garden for Abraham.
    Because unbelief arose again, it is I who lit the fire again.

9   With that Ḥallāj I used to say, "I am the Truth." Again it is I who placed the
    gallows rope on his neck.

10   When that beloved of God Muṣṭafā was going to start out on his Heavenly
       Ascent, that moment I humbled my soul, and it was I who perceived that
       mystery of His.

11   Now my name is Yūnus; at that time it was Ismāʿīl. It was I who, for that
       Beloved, becoming a sacrifice, ascended Mount Arafat.

12   The wheel of destiny is under my command, wherever I sit. Possessions and
       property are in my power; I am the one who burns them; I am the one
       who burns himself.

13   I am auspicious prosperity; I am happy. Yūnus also is with me. My master is
       the knowledge of the mysteries of God; I am that world of mysteries.

Halet Efendi, ff. 69a, 69b, 70a.

2   Fatih manuscript is not clear; could be *yıkan,* "one who destroys," or *yakan,* "one
       who burns."

4   *haẕret,* "presence of God" or "blessed man" (presumably Tapduk). Microcosm of the
       Whole refers to the belief that Man sums up the universe. He is connected both to
       the animal and to the spiritual world, and reflects within himself the divine attributes.

8   Nimrūd's fire (Kuran 21:69) refers to the story about the idolators (whose king is
       traditionally called Nimrūd) who threw Abraham into a fire, but God made the fire
       cool.

9   Hallāj (d. A.D. 922) was an early mystic who had an enormous influence on Islamic
       mysticism. He claimed to have reached union with the Divine Beloved. He became
       the symbol of the suffering martyr of love. He was executed for his famous
       statement: "anā'l-Haqq"—I am God, the Absolute Truth (Reality).

10   Muṣṭafā is another name for the Prophet. The Heavenly Ascent refers to his
       miraculous journey to the heavens.

13   *ol ʿalem-i esrār,* "that world of mysteries": reading from Halet Efendi, f. 70a.

CI

p. 93; ff. 129b, 130a

aldı benüm göñlümi noldugumı bilmezem

Meter: 7/7

1   He took my heart, I do not know what happened to me. I lost myself; [despite the fact that I went] searching, I cannot find [me].

2   I entered the road without a heart; my state is indescribable; I could not find a troubled one to tell my worries to for [even] a moment.

3   I am grateful; I met with my pain laughingly.(?) Although those afflicted with sorrow find [themselves], I [, however,] am unable to find myself.

4   If they say to me, "Who took your heart?" How can I tell [them]? I would cry and could not speak.

5   The whole world is filled with the One who took my heart. No matter where I look, I cannot see a place which is without Him.

6   I love the intoxication of love; I cannot be sober. Don't sit there sober; don't bring those without drinking vessels.(?)

7   The One who offers Yūnus the goblet is the One who says, "I am the Truth." He offered me a swallow; I drank [it]; I cannot be sober [again].

3   [Themselves] or [what they seek].

6   Reading *ayaq* for *ayag*.

CII

p. 93; ff. 130a, 130b

evvel benem āxır benem
cānlara cān olan benem

Meter: 8/8

1   I am the first and the last; I am the soul to the souls. I am the one who brings ready aid to those stranded on the Way.

2   I became stable. Who can perceive my secret? How will the one without eyes see me? I am the one who hid in the heart[s].

3   I am the one who became a drop at the moment of "Be!" who arranged the world at one look. I am the one who arranged the feast table through [my] exceptional power; I am the one who strikes the kettle drum of love.

4   I laid out these places [the earth] flat; I nailed in these mountains [to hold it down]. I made the sky into shades; it is I who grasp [the earth] and roll it up again [on the Last Day].

5   And, most wonderful, I also became one declaring religion and faith to the lovers. In the heart of the people I am misbelief, Islam, and belief.

6   Among the people, I am the one who arranges life, the one who wrote down the Four Books correctly. I am the one who writes black on white, who is the written Kuran.

7   I am the one who achieves Unity with the Beloved, who obeys [His] command, whatever it might be. I am that Gardener who adorns the realm and arranges the world.

8   I am the one who caused Ḥamza to go over the Qāf Mountains, who loosed his hand and foot. I am that poisonous snake behind the Sīmurg of the Qāf Mountains.

9   It is not Yūnus who is saying this; it is his Self saying this. He who doesn't believe this is a misbeliever: I am the Beginning and the End.

Halet Efendi, ff. 70a, 70b; R, f. 29.

2   "How," *kaçan,* as in the Fatih manuscript.

3   *Kun!* "Be!"; God's command in the Beginning which occasioned the creation of the world. The "feast table" refers to the *Bezm-ı Elast*, the Feast of "Am I not your Lord?" (Kuran 7:172). See Poem XCI, note to line 7.

4   Kuran 39:67, 78:7.

6   The Four Books are the Pentateuch, the New Testament, the Psalms, and the Kuran. These books were divinely transmitted to the prophets Moses, Jesus, David, and Muhammad, respectively.

7   Reading *bezeyüp*, "adorning," from Halet Efendi, f. 70b, instead of *yazayup*.

8   Qāf Mountains; See Poem IX, note 1. The Şīmurg is the fabulous bird that lives in the Qāf Mountains. Hamza was an uncle of the prophet, said to be very strong. In one of the legends about him, he was said to have been captured and carried off to the Qāf Mountains. In the end he succeeded in killing all his captors.

CIV

p. 94; ff. 131b, 132a, 132b

iy yārenler iy kardeşler

soruñ baña kandayıdum

Meter: 8/8

1   O lovers, O brothers, ask me where I was. Plunging into the sea of love, I was in the endless ocean.

2   He who guarded me, who preserved me wherever I was. . . . I was in the soul in the lantern at the tip of the wick of love.

3   Before the foundations of earth were laid, before earth and heavens were filled with creatures, before the Pen wrote on the Tablet, I was with the creator of the [whole] creation.

4   While one hundred and seventy thousand angels stood in rows, I saw Gabriel there, in that lofty council.

5   Before reading the Four Books, before there was separation and choice, I read my lessons, I was the reciter in the Kuran.

6   The hand of trouble cannot reach me; pain will never see me. I was at a lofty station beyond the evilness of worry.

7   While God was speaking ninety thousand divine words with His Beloved, the Prophet, and while thirty thousand were kept secret, at that time I was there.

8   If a hundred thousand wretched slaves of His like me should come, it would be little. My coming is now; in Paradise I was with Rıżvān.

9   I was a star for a long time; in the skies the angels were desirous [of me]. The all-compelling God commanded; I was There then.

10   Before I was in this form, when my name wasn't Yūnus, I was He, He was I; I was with the one who offered this love. (?)

Halet Efendi, ff. 71b, 72a; R, ff. 38, 39; TDTC, ff. 65a, 65b, 66a.

2   "Lantern . . . of love": According to Alevī-Bektaşī legends, God created a lantern to be the holy light (*nūr*) of Muḥammad and 'Alī (Gölpınarlı, *Yunus Emre . . . Dîvân*, p. 271).

3   "Before the Pen wrote on the Tablet," taking the Halet Efendi (f. 71b) version: *levhe kalem*.

4   Adding *anda*, "there," from Halet Efendi, f. 71b.

7   "Ninety thousand words": Muḥammad spoke this many words with God at the time of his Heavenly Ascent, *Mi'rāj*. Of these, he is said to have spoken thirty thousand to those of advanced spiritual understanding, and another thirty thousand he is said to have hidden and to have spoken only among the *ṣūfī*s.

8   "It would be little," i.e., many more should come. Rıżvān is the doorkeeper of Paradise.

10   "He was I": Fatih has *ol benidūm*, which is ungrammatical; it probably should read *ol benidi*. "I was with the one who offered": TDTC, f. 66a, has *sunandayıdum*, "I was in the one offering." Both Fatih and Halet Efendi have *sanandayıdum*.

CIX

p. 98; ff. 136a, 136b

hiç bilmezem kezek kimüñ aramuzda gezer ölüm

Meter: 8/8

1   I don't know at all whose turn it is; Death strolls about among us. He made the people [his] garden; Death plucks whom he wishes.

2   He ruins many a one; he destroys the property of many. He makes many shed tears; he destroys all their strength.

3   He takes the sibling of one; he cries a torrent of tears. The wound of his heart will never heal; Death comes without warning.

4   Death doesn't let a youth live until, growing to maturity, he knows himself. Laughing, leaving one he narrows his eyes, fixing them [upon others].

5   Where is his beloved Friend? Worship, go purely, wretched Yūnus; how can he endure [when] Death swallows [even] dragons?

2   "Ruins," *belini bükmek*, lit. "to bend double," "to weigh heavily on."

CXII

p. 101; ff. 141a, 141b

ben seni sevdügimi söyleşür(ler) hāş u 'amm

Meter: 7/7

1 Everybody talks about the fact that I love You. Let them who talk, talk; without You, life is forbidden [to me].

2 He whose soul has not tasted of Your sweetness is a walking soulless form, free of worry of the world.

3 I saw You just now, how can I be patient? All the world is desirous of seeing You for a moment.

4 What need of houris and castles [in Paradise] does he who sees You have? For him who doesn't love You, to his soul all places are Hell.

5 Even if I had the wealth of both worlds; without You, it is not fitting for me, for it is with You that [all] matters are complete.

6 If I had life of a thousand years, I'd spend it at this door. If I am a true lover, I must die on this road.

7 Many say to Yūnus, "What is the intoxication of love?" What should he do? The Pen wrote [his fate] in this way at the Primal Feast.

Halet Efendi, f. 79a.

7 *Ezel Bezmi* (*Bezm-i Alast*), the Primal Feast: see Poem XCI, note to line 7, and Poem CII, note to line 3.

CXIV

p. 102; ff. 142b, 143a

ben ol yarı sevdügümi nice bir gizleyübilem

Meter: 8/8

1   How can I hide the fact that I love that Beloved? My heart cannot contain [the secret]. What can I do unless I tell my secret?

2   The fact that I walk mutely is, they say, a sign of my feeling myself a stranger. I'll burn the veil of my strangeness and remove my veil.

3   I'll tell the worlds about my situation with Him. I'll shout [and] give the good news; I'll gather the world around me [to tell them].

4   The heart's eye of the lovers has gone toward the Beloved. I made an agreement with my heart; perhaps I'll reach the Beloved.

5   I would sacrifice my heart if He would accept it. [In any case] whenever it is to be, I am going to die; why should I then remain alive like this?

6   May thanks be to my soul if I should die for the Beloved. Everybody must die; where can I go [to escape] from death?

7   What Yūnus's tongue has said is not about knowledge and works. What can the tongue know about the Beloved and that I am one with the Beloved?

TDTC, ff. 132a, 132b.

6   A rhetorical question acknowledging there is nowhere to go to escape death.

CXVI

p. 103; ff. 143b, 144a, 144b

teferrüc eyleyü vardım şabāhın sinleri gördüm

Meter: 8/8

1   I strolled about in the morning; I saw the graves. I saw those delicate bodies, mixed with the black earth.

2   Bodies decayed [within] the earth, hidden inside the grave. I saw the emptied vein[s], flowed blood, shrouds soaked in blood.

3   I saw the ruined graves, filled up [with earth], all their houses ruined. All helpless from anxiety; what difficult states I saw!

4   The summer pastures no longer could be used as summer pastures; the winter pastures no longer could be used as winter pastures. I saw in mouth[s] tongues that had become rust-covered, that could no longer speak.

5   Some [taken by death while occupied] in pleasure and merrymaking, some [occupied] in music and [pleasure of] good news, some in torment; I saw days that had become nights.

6   Those black eyes had lost their luster; their moon faces had become blurred. Under the black earth I saw hands that arranged roses.

7   Some had bent their necks, flinging their bodies on the ground. Some had gone getting angry with their mothers; I saw destitute ones.

8   Some moaning, crying, the unfortunate ones burning with suffering. I saw their graves on fire, with smoke coming out.

9   Yūnus, when he saw this, came and told us about it: "My senses left me, my intellect was astounded, even as I saw these things."

2   Gölpınarlı adds *içre*, "within."

6   Taking Gölpınarlı's reading of *diren*, "arranged."

7   "Destitute ones," lit. "ones who had wrung their necks."

8   "Unfortunate ones . . .," lit. "flames brand their souls."

CXVII

p. 104; ff. 144b, 145a

ḥaqqdan baña naẓar oldı
ḥaqq kapusın açar oldum

Meter: 8/8

1   A glance fell on me from God; I began to be the opener of God's door. I began to enter God's treasury; I began to spread pearls and jewels.

2   The crown of prosperity was placed on [my] head. He offered me the glass of love; my soul drank; I was satiated with love. I began to be able to differentiate black from white.

3   It made me drunk, made me fall in love. I was raw; love cooked [me]. It brought my intellect [back to] my head; I began to be able to differentiate evil from good.

4   My affairs turned out well; my head became free from anxiety. I cut off the head of my carnal self; taking on wings, I began to fly.

5   Those who move from place to place reached the stopping place; they arrived and settled there. Life passed; the agreement was fulfilled; I turned [toward my goal]; I began to pass on.

6   Wretched Yūnus, ever since he became acquainted [with Tapduk] and gave his soul and heart; ever since I reached my Tapduk, I began to reveal my hidden secret.

5   *qarār itdi*, "they settled": Gölpınarlı adds *itdi*.

CXXVII

p. 109; ff. 151b, 152a

Ḥaq bir gevher yaratdı kendünüñ qudretinden

Meter: 7/7

1   From His own power, God created a jewel. He looked at the jewel; it melted because of awe of God.

2   He created seven levels of earth from that jewel's dust. He created seven levels of sky from that jewel's vapor.

3   He created seven seas from a drop of that jewel. He made firm the mountains from the foam of that sea.

4   He created Muḥammad because of his compassion for creatures. He also created ʿAlī because of his mercy for the Believers.

5   Who knows the matters of the Unseen World except through the knowledge of the Kuran? Yūnus drank and became drunk from the sea of that jewel.

CXXIX

p. 110; ff. 153a, 153b

iy dōst seni sevelden 'aqlum gitdi kaldum ben

Meter: 7/7

1   O Beloved, ever since I began loving, my intellect went away; I was left [without intellect]. Traveling the rivers, I plunged into the seas.

2   A particle of love's fire makes the seas boil; I fell into the fire of love; catching fire, I burned.

3   In that soul where love is, pain will not be. Ever since this love came to me, my pain has gone, I laughed.

4   And the nightingale fell in love with the red rose's face. I saw the face of those who arrived at the Divine Truth; I have become a nightingale.

5   You gave me this love, what should I do with myself? My interior and my exterior filled with light; I fell in love with the Beloved.

6   I was a dried-up tree, fallen on the road. The person skilled in mystical matters looked at me; I became fresh and young.

7   Yūnus, if you are a genuine lover, call yourself "Wretched." Preferring [it] to everything else, I found wretchedness.

R, ff. 53, 54.

CXXXI

p. 111; f. 154b

cānlar cañını buldum bu cānum yaġma olsun

Meter: 7/7

1   I found the soul of souls; let my soul be plundered. I passed beyond profit and loss; let my shop be plundered.

2   I passed beyond my "I-ness"; I opened the veil of my eye. I reached union with the Beloved; let my doubt be plundered.

3   I became sick of Duality; I became satiated at the tray of Unity. I drank the wine of pain; let my cure be plundered.

4   When wealth went traveling, the Friend came to us. The ruined heart filled with light; let my world be plundered.

5   I went beyond grief without end; I became sick of summer and winter. I found the best of the garden; let my garden be plundered.

6   Yūnus, how sweetly you spoke; you apparently ate honey and sugar. I found the honey of honeys; let my beehive be plundered.

Halet Efendi, ff. 81b, 82a.

2   "I passed beyond my 'I-ness'; I opened the veil of my eye": i.e., I went beyond the screen of carnal vision.

4   "When wealth went traveling" means "when I renounced worldly riches."

5   "Sick of . . . winter," i.e., sick of the relentless repetition of time, days, etc.

CXXXIV

pp. 112, 113; ff. 156b, 157a

'ilmünde ġarkolalı uş ben beni bilmezin

Meter: 7/7

1   Since I've been drowned in Your knowledge, I don't know me. I cannot, speaking with the tongue, describe You.

2   One cannot express Your aspect; who knows Your whereabouts? I'm not at all worthy of relating Your deeds with my tongue.

3   You are both the First and the Last; You are present everywhere. There is no place without You; why can't I see You?

4   Without seeing You, I became mad [with love]; I erred; I committed sins. I let my sense and intellect be taken away; I became drunk; I won't become sober.

5   Since You made me drunk, and took away my soul and heart, don't take me away from You; I have found [You]; I won't leave.

6   You gave me soul; You commanded 'Azrā'īl; I'll deliver up my soul; I won't make false claims.

Note: It is unusual that Yūnus did not include his name in the last verse.

CXXXV

p. 113; ff. 157a, 157b; ff. 83b, 84a

'āşıqlara ne diyem 'ışq xaberinden şīrīn

Meter: 7/7

1   What can I tell the lovers that is sweeter than news of love? I will explain it one by one to those who listen with love.

2   Before when there was no earth or sky, there was the foundation of love. Love is very ancient, eternal; love brought about everything there is.

3   At the Primal Feast, at the beginning of Time, whoever saw the Beloved's face his soul was in love; ask him for news of love.

4   No matter what I try to liken love to, it doesn't work. In this world and the next, what can take love's place!

5   It is entrusted [to you], guard well the news of love! Do not sit just anywhere and speak about love.

6   This is the rule among the money changers: they do not show the jewels to those who don't know their worth.

7   Yūnus's intellect is filled with love. He cannot hide his pains; he cannot help himself from speaking the language of love.

Halet Efendi, ff. 83b, 84a.

3   *Ezel Bezmi*: See Poem XCI, at note 7.

6   "They do not," lit. "they did not."

7   "He cannot hide," lit. "he could not hide."

CXLI

p. 116; ff. 160b, 161a, 161b

ḥaqdan gelen şerbeti içdük elḥamdulillāh

Meter: 7/7

1 Of the wine which flows from God, we have drunk; praise be to God!
We have crossed this great sea of power; praise be to God!

2 These mountains, oak forests, and vineyards opposite
With good health and peace of mind we have passed over; praise be to God!

3 We were dried out, we became fresh; we've grown wings, we've become
birds.
We've become equal, one to another; we have flown; praise be to God!

4 To the countries where we've gone, to those pure hearts [filled with affection]
We have spread Tapduk's inner truth to the people; praise be to God!

5 Come here and let's make peace; if you're a stranger, let's get acquainted.
Our horses were saddled up, we rode out; praise be to God!

6 We went down to Rūm for the winter months, [where] we did much good and
bad.
Then when spring returned, we moved on; praise be to God!

7 Spring by spring we collected together, we became a river;
We flowed down into the sea, overflowed; praise be to God!

8 In the presence of Tapduk we were servants at his door.
Wretched Yūnus had been raw, now he's cooked; praise be to God!

Note: This poem, with its refrain "praise be to God," was probably used in the ṣūfī
ceremonies. It also contains interesting references to a nomadic raiding life (ll. 5-7),
reminiscent of the Ottomans' early nomadic life.

6 Rūm is central Anatolia or the Byzantine Empire; later used to refer to the Balkans.

8 "Raw," i.e., spiritually untrained.

CLV

p. 123; ff. 171a, 171b

bīmekānum bu cihānda
menzilüm turaġum anda

Meter: 8/8

1 I am without a halting place in this world; my stopping place is There. I am a sultan whose throne and crown, dress of Paradise, and Burāq are There.

2 I am Job; I found this patience; I am Jerjis; I died a thousand times. I came to this dominion alone; all my supplies are There.

3 I am a nightingale; I came singing. I came holding the royal patent on my tongue. I came here to sell my musk; I am a deer; my grazing place is There.

4 Who knows what kind of bird I am? I am companion to that moon-faced one. I have been drunk since Eternity; I have drunk; my drinking vessel is There.

5 I am mad; I won't heed advice; I won't go to just any ordinary place. Look, I won't heed these words, but my ear is There.

6 One doesn't divulge secret words; There water isn't burned by fire. It burns night and day; it doesn't go out; my lamp is There.

7 I have wandered up and down this realm; I have strolled around seven times. I have seen the Light of Muḥammad; it is mine; my place is There.

8 Yūnus, you have become absorbed in this thought, and tossed the world behind you. By God! [My palate] received a pleasant flavor; my palate was filled [with a pleasant flavor] There.

Halet Efendi, ff. 95a, 95b, 96a.

CLIX

p. 125; ff. 173b, 174a

saña direm iy velī tur irte namāzına

Meter: 7/7

1   I say to you, O friend of God, rise for the morning prayer. If you aren't dead, rise for the morning prayer.

2   The muezzin recites the call for prayer, he calls out God's name. Do not destroy the foundations of religion; rise for the morning prayer.

3   Birds rise on wings; the trees toll their beads. Brothers who receive miraculous support from the saint[s], rise for the morning prayer.

4   Perform your prayer with litanies of praise; raise your hands in thanks. With the thought that you are going to die, rise for the morning prayer.

5   Perform your prayers so that you will have provisions, so that you will have what you need in the next life. So that it will be a lamp in your grave, rise for the morning prayer.

6   Perform your prayers with the *imām*; do not lie down in doubt. So that you will go with faith, rise for the morning prayer.

7   The soul will leave [the body] and go away, too, and the body will remain, too. Dervish Yūnus, you also, rise for the morning prayer.

Note: This poem is similar in style and content to the poem by Aḥmed Yesevī mentioned in the note to Poem XXXIX.

1   *velī*, "friend of God," also "companion," "saint," "spiritually advanced."

3   "Trees toll their beads," i.e., rustle and murmur as if repeating their prayers.

CLXVIII

p. 130; ff. 180b. 181a

baña namāz kılmaz dime
ben bilürem namāzumı

Meter: 8/8

1   Do not say about me, "He doesn't perform his prayers." I know my prayers. Whether I perform them or don't perform them, God knows my supplication.

2   Other than the Beloved, no one knows who is a Muslim and who a misbeliever. I would pray if God accepted my unorthodox behavior.

3   That behavior is accepted in God's court; he [who behaves that way] drinks from the wine of the spiritual realm. It opens the eye of the soul, without a veil. The Beloved himself wipes [away the veil from] my eye.

4   The Friend is here; clear and evident; I saw the Beloved's face plainly. He who studies knowledge and mystical learning—their purpose is this.

5   The ordinary lover who cannot always find the Beloved's road, who cannot explain the secret spiritual meaning, will not explain this hidden secret of mine.

6   Achieve [comprehension of] the essence of my words; give news of that which is without sign or indication. Ask the troubled lovers about these pain-filled messages of mine.

7   Pain is the remedy for the lover; the lovers full of pain are wealthy. Those who listen to my words say it is the voice of dignity and strength.

8   He who is searching for the Beloved should come to me; I will show the Beloved to him. This is my total speech: "I know myself."

9   Yūnus, now speak of God, let them consider you an unbeliever even. God's food is cooking; let those learned in mystical matters taste my salt.

2   *nāz*, "whim," "unorthodox behavior." Gölpınarlı (*Yūnus Emre . . . Dîvân*, p. 282) says *nāz* is one of the attributes of God's beloveds, who at times say and do things which appear inappropriate or unpleasant. Such people base their belief on the *hadīth* that says that if God loves one of his servants, [the servant's] sin will not affect him.

8   *öñden soña*, "total[ly]." See *Yūsuf-i Meddāḥ, Varqa ve Gülşāh*, ed. Grace Martin Smith (Leiden, 1976), vv. 101, 910. "I know myself" refers to the *ḥadīth* "He who knows himself knows his Lord."

CLXXIII

p. 133; ff. 184a, 184b

kaçan [kim]ol dilber benüm
göz[lerü]me tudaş oldı

Meter: 8/8

1   When my eyes fell upon that Beauty, He took away my senses, intellect, and became a traveling companion to my heart.

2   My heart says, "I am His slave"; my soul says, "I am His slave." I don't know at all to whom it belongs; between [my heart and soul] a quarrel arose.

3   I realized that between them was my success. Although there was no conversation [between us], I became pleased with [the Beauty].

4   Wherever I should look, He is the one who comes before my eye, before me, behind me, on my right, my left; it became spring although it was winter.

5   Although I was not Khızır and İlyās, I met eternal life. Although never eating and drinking, my inside became filled with food.

6   His love is in the hearts of the whole world. Who doesn't love Him with his soul, know that his belief is a stone.

7   May the fire from your love not fly out and land upon anyone! A particle touched Yūnus; it became revealed [throughout] the world.

TDTC, f. 79b.

5   Khızır and İlyās: Khızır, a shadowy figure mentioned in the Kuran, is known in particular as one who found eternal life. İlyās is said to have gone with Khızır and to have also found and drunk from the Fountain of Life. Once a year, on the morning of Hıdrellez (Khızır-İlyās) Day, they meet at a rosebush. Khızır helps those in trouble on land, and İlyas those at sea.

CLXXIV

p. 133; ff. 185a, 185b, 186a

yir gök yaradılmadan Ḥaq bir gevher eyledi

Meter: 7/7

1   Before earth and sky were created, God made a jewel. He regarded the jewel, [but His look couldn't be] contained by the jewel, [so] it revolved.

2   Moisture came out of the jewel; from that moisture He created the sky. As decoration for the sky, He made many stars.

3   He said to the sky: "Turn!" "The moon and sun should move," He said. He suspended the water and made the top of it land.

4   The earth tossed about; it didn't stop; it wasn't settled for a moment. God made the great mountains [as] spikes to hold the earth in place.

5   'Azrā'īl descended to earth; [God] took a handful of earth; He kneaded four angels; He made a prophet.

6   When the soul entered the body, it sneezed and stood up. At that moment he lifted his hands and thanked God.

7   God says to Adam, "[Be] thankful you reached this moment. What did you perceive in this world? Why did your tongue speak?"

8   [Adam:] "When there was nothing You created [me], when I was earth, You gave [me] a soul. You spoke with the tongue of power; You made my tongue speak."

9   This speech pleased God; He made His servant noble. Whatever occurred to Him, He gave [Adam]; He prepared [it for Adam].

10   Where do these words to Yūnus come from? He will tell [us] from his heart. It seems that the grace of the King looked upon him.

115

TDTC, ff. 94, 95.

5   'Azrā'īl is generally the Angel of Death. Here Yūnus refers to God's sending him to earth to find earth from which God was to fashion Adam. The four angels are Jibrīl, Mīhā'īl, Isrāfīl, and 'Azrā'īl.

6   TDTC, f. 95, has *ol demde* "at that moment" instead of *şolqadar*.

CLXXIX

pp. 137, 138; ff. 190b, 191a, 191b

ol çalabun 'ışqı benüm baġrum baş eyledi

Meter: 7/7

1   God's love wounded my breast. It took my heart and revealed my secret.

2   It will never leave [my] heart, will never be missing from my tongue. God brought His light to my eye.

3   The eye of [my] soul saw [God's light]; [my] tongue gave news [of it]. It dwelled within [my] soul; it made my heart its throne.

4   He offered a goblet to [my] soul; [my] soul drank to repletion. The drinking cup came full; it intoxicated [my] soul.

5   Our soul became drunk; our tongue began to pour forth pearls [elegant speech]. That love of my God made me drunk.

6   When can I be a dervish so that I may be a friend to Him? Love made a hundred thousand like me put on the dervish cloak.

7   Yūnus now is consoled; he is pleased; he saw the Beloved. Yūnus revels in the company of those spiritually advanced, [inspired by the power of] love.

R, f. 75.

1   R has *Haq çalabuñ 'ışqı baġrumı baş eyledi*, "God's love wounded my breast." As Gölpınarlı notes, the first line has one too many feet; he suggests eliminating *ol*, "that," which I have done.

117

CLXXXII

p. 139; ff. 192b, 193a

toldur bize [sun] qadeḥi 'ışq şarābından iy sāqī

Meter: 8/8

1   Fill the goblet, O cupbearer, with the wine of love, and offer [it to us].   Let us drink from that sea from which sheikhs and learned men drink.

2   Our conversation is divine; our words are the waters of Kevser.   Our King is the King of Kings; our instrumental music is about the grief of separation from the Beloved.

3   Every moment there will be pleasant conversation; the *muftī* and the university professor will be checkmated [by its superiority].   It is a divine prosperity; whoever drinks from it will be eternal.

4   A dervish cloak and crown do not open the Way; one doesn't become a scholar by wearing a ceremonial cloak; religion and piety will not come [to You] even if You read all the folios [of the religious books].

5   You have read seven texts; oh yes, [your] worship exhibits purity.   But since you have not performed any [good] deeds, if necessary go, study, for a hundred years [more].

6   Even if you have gone on the Pilgrimage a thousand times, have fought holy wars a thousand times—if you have broken a heart [just] once, if necessary go traveling [continuously] from now on [in atonement]. (?)

7   Tell me, clever one, which is better, the heart or the Ka'be?   The heart is, because the stopping place of the Beloved is in the heart.

8   God has entrusted the hearts of those close to Him to the Prophet; on the night of the Heavenly Ascent, these words became eternalized with the Beloved.

9   Yūnus, this is your duty: take hold of the skirts of the "Hearts" if you wish to be eternal, [since] hearts are eternal.

R, ff. 81, 82.

1   "Offer," adding *sun*.

2   "Our instrumental music . . ." is similar to the opening of Rūmī's six-volume mystical poem, the *Mesnevī*:

> . . . Listen to the reed how it tells a tale, complaining of separations—
> Saying, "Ever since I was parted from the reed-bed, my lament hath caused man and woman to moan.
> I want a bosom torn by severance, that I may unfold [to such a one] the pain of love desire."
> (*The Mathnawī of Jalālu'ddīn Rūmī*, ed. Reynold A. Nicolson [London, 1977], vol. 2, p. 5)

3   Taking the R version: "*her bir demde sohbet ola. . . .*"

4   The *ferej* is a cloak worn by the *'ulemā'*, the religious class, on ceremonial occasions. The *tāj* is a type of "[dervish] headgear" (or read *hāj*, "cross"?).

5   "Seven texts" refers to the seven different ways of reading the Kuran. There are *hadīth*s which say the Kuran is read in seven different ways, without any change in meaning. The *sūfī*s consider these seven different styles as representing seven different meanings (A.Gölpınarlı (*Yunus Emre. . .Dîvân*, p. 298).

9   "Hearts," i.e., those close to God.

CLXXXVI

p. 141; ff. 195a, 195b, 196a

ben bende seyrideriken 'aceb sırra irdüm ahī

Meter: 8/8; 4 müstef'ilün

1   As I was strolling around in myself, what a wonder—I learned a secret, friend; and you, you also see Him in yourself: I saw the Beloved in me, friend.

2   I looked at myself; I saw in myself the one who is one with me. I know who is the soul to my form; I found out, friend.

3   Searching I could not find out if He were I, or where I am. I couldn't distinguish me from Him; all of a sudden I became Him!

4   My heart won't accept the one who says "form is [made of] earth." I made the essence of this earth reach God, friend.

5   The unbeliever won't perceive this, [but] the heart[s] of the afflicted ones will perceive this. I am the nightingale of the garden of love; I came from that garden, friend.

6   The Beloved is with us; he's not as separated [from us] as one hair is from another. We are spared distant journeys [since] I found the Beloved close by, friend.

7   Why should I travel just any road? I'll not scatter in just any direction. My journey became fortunate; I reached a pleasant, mystical station.

8   In the beginning of time I was Manṣūr; that's why I came here. Burn [me]; toss my ashes to the sky; I became "I am God," friend.

9   I'll neither burn and [my ashes] be scattered, nor mount the gallows and be hanged. When my work is finished, I'll walk about, [since] I came here to stroll around and divert myself, friend.

10   Being destitute, I became affluent; the universe became mine. [Everywhere] from the earth to the sky, [from] the west [to] the east, I filled earth and sky, friend.

11   Just as I found myself, this happened: I found God! I was afraid until I found Him; I have been saved from fear, friend.

12   Yūnus, who kills you? The one who gives the soul will take it again. I learned who it is who rules these souls, friend.

TDTC, ff. 155b, 156a.

1   "Secret," or "mystery," reading *sırra* from TDTC, f. 156a.

8   This verse and verse 9 refer to Manṣūr al-Ḥallāj (see note to line 9 of Poem C). After he was hanged and decapitated, he was burned, and his ashes were thrown into the Tigris.

CLXXXVIII

p. 142; ff. 197a, 197b

işidün ey yārenler eve dervīşler geldi

Meter: 7/7

1   Listen, O dear friends, dervishes have come to the house! Let's give our souls
     with deep thanks; dervishes have come to the house!

2   Whoever sees their faces abases himself. He sings of the hidden, spiritual
     wisdom; dervishes have come to the house!

3   Dervishes are flying birds; they winter by the edge of the sea. [They have]
     very auspicious heads; dervishes have come to the house!

4   The dervishes have fresh and lovely faces; those who see them become mad
     [with love and delight]. Their hidden [selves] are grander than the Throne;
     dervishes have come to the house!

5   They came from the land of Seydī Balum, sugar dripping from their tongues.
     By way of the road of the garden of the Beloved, dervishes have come to
     the house!

6   Yūnus, your slave is without a confidant; he has no one; he is all alone. May
     your soul be sacrificed; dervishes have come to the house!

3   God/the Truth is often symbolized as the sea.

5   According to one source, Seydī Balum was a prince from the house of Germiyan, an
     early Turkish principality. This shadowy figure has also been associated with a very
     early religious figure, Geyikli Baba.

p. 143; ff. 198b, 199a

menzil irāq bu yoluñ bu yola kim varası

Meter: 7/7

1   The stages of this road are far away; who will [be able to] go? There are many difficulties on this road; who will succeed?

2   Arms and supplies are necessary on this road; few [provisions (?)] are necessary; many [spiritual provisions (?)] are necessary. A good, iron heart is necessary to go on this difficult road.

3   On the road, they say, its character is the narrow bridge, Şırāṭ [which leads from this world to Paradise]. The means [to cross the Şırāṭ bridge] for the person who is going to the Beloved is following the Straight Path.

4   God loves whoever is Righteous. That spiritual man's [spiritual] capital is worthy of the two worlds.

5   The catapult of Righteousness with the stone of "asking for God's pardon" went straight on, was thrown, and the fortress of the carnal self collapsed.

6   Know that on this road there are many who play tricks on [your] faith. The dishonor of those who follow their baser instincts will never go away.

7   Know there are one hundred thousand armies of hypocrisy on this road. A spiritually "arrived" man who has killed his carnal self is required to rout this army.

8   Yūnus now is inviting: "Come, let's go to non-existence [i.e., Fenā']. If your eyes are suitable, you will see the Beloved's face."

R, f. 78.

2   Taking the Ritter version (f. 78): *bu yola yarak gerek, eksük gerek, çok gerek.*

3   The Şırāṭ bridge: See Poem XII, note to line 7.

CXCIV

p. 145; ff. 201b, 202a

'ışquñ aldı benden beni baña seni gerek seni

Meter: 8/8

1 Love for You took me from myself; it is You I need, You. I burn for You both night and day; it is You I need, You.

2 I take no joy in worldly wealth, nor feel dismay at poverty. I am content with Your love; it is You I need, You.

3 Their love of You destroys [Your] lovers; it plunges them in love's sea. It fills them with the sight of You; it is You I need, You.

4 If I were intoxicated by love's wine, and should become mad and destitute, my concern would be of You night and day; it is You I need, You.

5 The mystics need their gatherings for conversation; the brothers need the other world. Majnūns need [their] Leyla; it is You I need, You.

6 If they should kill me and fling my ashes to the sky, my dust would cry there, "It is You I need, You."

7 Yūnus Emre is my name; my fire increases day by day. In the two worlds my goal is this: it is You I need, You.

5   ahī, "brothers," referring here to members of fraternal-religious trade guild groups, present in Anatolia in the Middle Ages; discussed by Ibn Baṭṭūṭa. See *The Travels of Ibn Baṭṭūṭa*, ed. H. A. R. Gibb (Cambridge, 1962), vol. 2, pp. 418-22. Majnūn, Leyla: prototypical lovers (see Poem VI).

7   "Two worlds," i.e., this world and the next.

CXCIX

p. 148; ff. 204b, 205a, 205b

'ömrüm beni sen aldaduñ

ah nideyin 'ömrüm seni

Meter: 8/8; 4 müstef'ilün

1   My life, you deceived me; O my life, what should I do with you! You made me unable to move; O my life, what should I do with you!

2   My being used to be totally you; you were the soul within my soul. And you were sultan to me; O my life, what should I do with you!

3   I used to console my heart with you; I used to sniff you, saying, "[This is a] rose." Feeling homesick and lonely I used to cry; O my life, what should I do with you!

4   Whoever comes here goes, they say; the affairs of the world are all a lie. Who loses his life, weeps; O my life, what should I do with you!

5   My good [deeds] and my evil [deeds] will be written down. The thread of my life will be snapped. Departing, the form will be ruined; O my life, what should I do with you!

6   At least if you would only not get up and flee, and wouldn't move from place to place like a nomad, if only you wouldn't drink the wine of death; O my life, what should I do with you!

7   One day I'll be left without you; I'll be a meal for the worms and the birds; rotting, I'll become earth; O my life, what should I do with you!

8   Wretched Yūnus, don't you know [this] or won't you see? Won't you think about the dead? O my life, what should I do with you!

5   Everyone's deeds will be written down at the Final Reckoning.

7   *kurd kuş*, "worms and the birds," "wild beasts" (Robert Dankoff, written communication).

CCII

p. 150; ff. 207a, 207b

geldi geçdi 'ömrüm benüm
şol yil esüp geçmiş gibi

Meter: 8/8

1   My life came and passed like that wind, blew and passed on. Indeed, it seemed to me as if I [just] opened and shut [my] eye [and it passed].

2   Look, God is witness to these words: this soul is [only] a guest in this body. One day it will leave it and go away, as a bird flown away from the nest.

3   They likened the wretched son of Adam to a farmer: some grow, some die—like the seeds he cast upon the ground.

4   There is one thing that makes my interior burn, my self burn [with anguish]: those who die young, as if [the farmer] reaped the crop [when] unripe.

5   If you have called upon a sick person, given someone a drink of water, tomorrow, there [in the next world] he will come to meet [you] as if he had drunk God's wine.

6   If you have seen an unfortunate one, and given him an old piece of clothing, tomorrow [he will meet you as if he had put on a heavenly robe].

7   Yūnus Emre, they say two people will remain in this world: it turns out it will be Khıżır and İlyās, as they have drunk from the Water of [Eternal] Life.

6   Fatih has "as if he had drunk the wine of God." This is probably a scribal error (cf. line 5). The second half of the verse should be something like "he will meet you as if he had put on a heavenly robe."

7   Khıżır and İlyās: See Poem CLXXIII, note to line 5.

CCIII

p. 150; ff. 208a, 208b, 209a, 209b

yā ilāhī ger su'āl itseñ baña
cevābum işbuyıdı anda sana

Meter: 7/4; fāʻīlātün fāʻīlātün fāʻīlāt

1   O God, if You should question me, this would be my answer to it:

2   I treated myself cruelly; I sinned. What did I do to You, O King?

3   Before I came, You said my right share was bad; before I was [even] born, You said, "Adam is very rebellious."

4   [If] You have written me down as "rebellious from eternity," You will fill the world with the resulting clamor [of my behavior]. (?)

5   Was it I who fashioned me? [No], it was *You* who fashioned me. Why did You create me filled with faults, O One Without Needs!

6   I opened my eyes and the inside of the prison I saw was filled with the carnal self and desires and filled with devils.

7   Let me not die in prison; open up! A number of times I have eaten some pure things as well as some unclean things.

8   What decreased from Your realm? Did my authority take precedence over Yours?

9   Did I eat my daily bread and [thus] leave You hungry? Or did I eat Your meal and leave You in need?

10   You stretch a bridge like a hair, saying, "Pass over. Come, so that you may release yourself from My trap."

11   Can a man pass over a bridge like a hair? Either he'll fall or manage to hang on or fly.

12   Your slaves make a bridge for good [purposes]. The good is so that they may pass over [or] for an excursion.

13   It is necessary even that its foundations be firm, so that those passing over will say, "This is the Straight Path."

14   You set up a scale to weigh [my] whims and desires; You intend to throw me into the fire.

15   A scale is necessary for him who is a grocer or else a merchant, a trader, or a druggist.

16   Since sin is the most unclean thing of unclean things, it is a matter not befitting Your majesty.

17   You ought to conceal it with kindness. So, what need is there for You to reveal the uncleanness and weigh it?

18   You will watch as I burn merrily. Heaven forbid [that should happen], O God of Mankind!

19   You are all-seeing; You indeed know my state; so what need have You to weigh my deeds?

20   [After] having killed me, making me rot, filling my eye with dirt, hasn't Your [need for taking] revenge passed?

21   No harm came to You from Yūnus. You know that which is evident and that which is hidden.

22   So many dry words for a [mere] handful of earth. Why is that necessary, O kind and glorious God?

Note: This poem is written in the form of a *meṣnevī* (couplets with different rhymes but one meter throughout) and is, according to Gölpınarlı, a fine example of the *ṣatḥ / ṣatḥıyye* form. In one type of this form the poet, or shaman, is in a kind of trance when he recites and is unaware of what he says. However, this poem represents the second kind of *ṣatḥıyye*, in which the poet is aware of what he says and uses the poem to express his own wishes. *Ṣūfī*s call this latter kind of poetry *nāz* and those who recite it "people of contempt or disdain (*nāz*)." This form is very prevalent among the Bektaṣī order of dervishes.

3–5   "Adam is very rebellious": Gölpınarlı believes Yūnus was referring to the whole of mankind, and in particular to himself. Yūnus says that both his inclination toward good and his inclination toward evil come from God. He seems to have forgotten that life is a place of trial.

6 "Prison": Gölpınarlı says this refers to the *ḥadīth* that says the world is a prison for the believer and paradise for the misbeliever.

6–22 Yūnus, one whose "faith is complete," in this section of the poem feigns disdain and acts in a contemptuous manner toward God. Gölpınarlı believes that this poem was the inspiration for the fifteenth-century poet Kaygusuz Abdal's poem beginning "*Yücelerden yüce gördüm erbabsın sen Koca Tanrı*" (A. Gölpınarlı, *Alevî-Bektaşî Nefesleri* [Istanbul, 1963], 14–15, 213).

13 "The Straight Path": See Poem CXC, note to line 3.

22 Redhouse (1890), p. 1419, gives "tittle tattle" for *qıl u qāl*.

Additional Poems

These poems are not in the Fatih manuscript
but are cited by Gölpınarlı.

XXXVIII

p. 173

Meter: 8/8

1   Let's not be satisfied with one glance; come, let's go to the Beloved, Heart! Let's not die with the pain of longing due to separation; come, let's go to the Beloved, Heart!

2   Come, let's go, before the soul rises, before leaving the body. Before the enemy enters, come, let's go to the Beloved, Heart!

3   Come, let's go, don't stay far off; for the Beloved let's make preparations for the road. The halting place is in the presence of the sheikh; come, let's go to the Beloved, Heart!

4   Let's leave country and town; let's weep for the Beloved. Let's take the Beloved into [our] hands; come, let's go to the Beloved, Heart!

5   Let's not stay in this world; it's transitory; let's not be deceived. Since we're one, let's not separate; come, let's go to the Beloved, Heart!

6   Let's pass through this world; let's fly to the land of that Beloved. Let's give up desire and passion; let's go to the Beloved, Heart!

7   Be my guide; let's head toward the Beloved. Let's not look either backward or forward; let's go to the Beloved, Heart!

8   This world will not be lasting; open your eye; arouse your soul. Be to me traveling companion and lover; come, let's go to the Beloved, Heart!

9   Before the word of death comes, before Death takes [us by] our collars, before 'Azrā'il strikes, come, let's go to the Beloved, Heart!

10   Let's reach the genuine person [who has arrived at the Divine Truth]; let's ask for information about God. Let's take Yūnus Emre; come, let's go the Beloved, Heart!

From additional poems, not in Fatih.

133

LXXI

p. 190

Meter: 8/8

1   Again you have overflowed, mad heart. Will you burble like the water?
Again you have flowed, my bloody tears. Will you block my way[s]?

2   What should I do? I can't reach the Beloved; there is no remedy to be found
for my pain. I have become a wanderer [far] from my land. Will you
delay me here?

3   I lost my traveling companion; the wound of my breast cannot be healed.
Bloody tears from my eyes! Will you become a river and splash?

4   I have become dust on your path; you protect me exceedingly well. Are you
those stone-breasted mountains over there, swelling their breasts across
from me?

5   Snowy mountain! Coming down on my road like a robber. I have been
separated from my Beloved. Will you bar my way?

6   Cloud, hanging in clusters on the head of the snowy mountains, will you let
down your hair and secretly weep for me?

7   Yūnus's soul has become drunk; I'm on the road. Where are my lands?
Yūnus saw you in his dream. Are you sick? Are you well?

From additional poems, not in Fatih.

LXXII

p. 190

Meter: 8/8

1   I wonder would there be someone as wretched as I, with wounded breast, and weeping eye, as wretched as I.

2   I wander around Anatolia, Syria, the Upper Lands—all. I searched very much, but I could not find someone as wretched as I.

3   May no one be wretched; may they not burn in the fire of longing. My teacher, let no one be as wretched as I.

4   My tongue speaks; my eye weeps; my inner self burns for the wretched ones. It seems in the sky my star is as wretched as I.

5   I'll burn so much with this pain, one day the appointed hour of death will come; I'll die, and surprisingly enough, in my grave I'll find someone as wretched as I.

6   They'll say, "A wretch died"; three days later [the rest of the people] will hear [the news]. They'll wash [me] with cold water, as wretched as I.

7   Hey, my Lover Yūnus, unfortunate one! No cure can be found for my pain. Go, now, travel about from city to city as wretched as I.

From additional poems, not in Fatih.

1   "Wretched," also "homeless, lonely, away from home."

2   Gölpınarlı says the Alevīs and the Bektaşīs refer to Azerbaijan and Iran as the Upper Lands.

LXXIV

pp. 191, 192

ilāhī bir 'ışq ver baña kandalıgum bilmeyeyin

Meter: 8/8

1 My God! Give me a love so that I won't know where I am. Let me lose myself; seeking, let me not find myself.

2 Make me so amazed that I won't know day from night. May I always seek You, and no longer remain [at the stage of] external form.

3 Take away, remove from me "I-ness"; fill me with "You-ness." Kill me in Your Life, so that I won't go There and die.

4 If to my burning tongue should come [the names of those] who curse me, who laugh at me, at least let me burn with its pain [of knowing that]; let me not speak about my state.

5 Look, I'm walking along burning, my liver sunk in blood. Love completely affected [my] soul; how can I not wail?

6 My heart perceived Your aroma; it renounced the world. Your location will never be visible; where should I seek You?

7 Let me be a nightingale and sing; let me lie down in the garden of the Friend. Becoming a rose, let me open, and let me not fade any more.

8 Like Manṣūr [take] me to the gallows; clearly show [me] Yourself. May I sacrifice this soul; may I not be a denier of love.

9 Love is the remedy for pain; I laid down my life for the sake of love. Yūnus Emre says this, "Let me not be without love for a moment."

From additional poems, not in Fatih.

5 Reading *tap*, "completely," instead of *tup*.

8 Manṣūr: See Poem C, note to line 9.

LXXVI

pp. 192, 193

iy yārenler iy kardaşlar
korkaram ben ölem diyü

Meter: 8/8

1   O beloved ones, O brothers, I'm afraid because I'll die. I'm not concerned about my dying [but rather] that I'll find [There] what [sins] I committed [in this life].

2   One day I will appear to my eyes; my fault[s] will strike [me] in the face. I've become mad from worry, thinking about what I should do—what should I do?

3   If I were a true slave, I would have performed the services of a slave for Him. I would have wept in this world, so that tomorrow I might laugh There [in the next world].

4   In the same way I came to this world, enslaved to my carnal passions. I did no good works, [not thinking] that I might be spared torture [in the next world].

5   O powerless, wretched Yūnus, you have my sins; what should you do? [Yūnus:] "I took refuge in that God of mine, and He said, 'I'll pardon [you].' "

From additional poems, not in Fatih.

XCV

p. 202

Meter: 8/8

1   I wander, burning; love dyed me with blood. I am neither rational nor mad; come see what love has done to me.

2   Sometimes I blow like the wind; sometimes I raise dust like the roads. Sometimes I flow like the floods; come see what love has done to me.

3   I murmur like flowing streams; I brand my pain-laden liver. Thinking of my sheikh I cry; come see what love has done to me.

4   Either take my hand and raise me up, or let me achieve union with you. You have made me cry much; [now] make me laugh; come see what love has done to me.

5   I walk from land to land; I ask after the sheikh in various languages. Who knows my state in exile from my native land? Come see what love has done to me.

6   Becoming Majnūn I wander; I see that Beloved in a dream. I awake and become sad; come see what love has done to me.

7   I am wretched, poor Yūnus, covered with wounds from head to toe. I am a wanderer separated from the land of the Beloved; come see what love has done to me.

From additional poems, not in Fatih.

5   "I ask . . . languages," or "I question everyone I meet."

Glossary

'Abdurrezzāq - Also known as Sheikh-i San'ān, a sheikh who sees himself in a dream worshipping an idol. To understand his dream, he sets out on a journey with four hundred disciples. When they reach Anatolia, he sees a Christian woman with whom he falls in love. He puts on the Christian girdle, one of the symbols used for Christians, and, at the suggestion of the woman, worships idols. The sheikh's disciples, having no success in getting the sheikh to give up the woman and these abhorrent practices, go on the Pilgrimage. At Mecca they, along with another dervish, pray for the sheikh. This dervish sees Muḥammad in a dream and learns that the sheikh has become Muslim again. The woman also has a dream. She follows the sheikh and his disciples and, upon reaching them, becomes Muslim and dies. (LXVIII)

ahī - Member of a religiously oriented trade guild.

aloes tree - A fragrant wood often used for incense. (XLI)

'arūż - Quantitative meter.

'āşıq - Folk poet, minstrel; lover (of God).

attribute (*şifat*) - A philosophical concept that occasioned much discussion. The various religious and philosophical schools held different positions on "attribute." According to the *şūfī*s, all attributes are attributes of God; one should not separate the essence, or substance, from the attribute. (LXVIII)

'Azāzīl - The Devil, Satan, İblis. (XLI)

'Azrā'īl - The Angel of Death. (XC, XCIV)

bahrī - Kingfisher, sea bird; also mariner, sailor. (XCI)

berāt - Official document written in the *dīvānī* script, stamped with the *tuġrā* (the Sultan's monogram). It states the name and place of service of one appointed to a position and the income and duties associated with that position. (XXXVI)

Bezm-i Elast - See "Ezel Bezmi." (CII)

Bridge - See "Ṣırāṭ."

Burāq - The miraculous winged steed Muḥammad rode on his Heavenly Ascent (*Mir'āj*) usually pictured as having a human face. (XXXI, XCIX)

cruelty - God's hiding himself from a devotee. (XXVI)

dervish - Member of a religious order founded on the teaching of an influential man of piety (see n. 4 to the Introduction).

eighteen rivers - Refers to the eighteen worlds that make up the universe according to ancient belief. These include Universal Reason, Universal Soul, the nine heavens, the four elements (air, fire, water, earth), and the three kingdoms (animal, vegetable, mineral). (XCIV)

Ezel Bezmi - The Primal Feast, based on Kuran 7:171. The echo of the oath of loyalty sworn by man to God at that feast impels the soul to the search for the Truth. The day of the creation of man. (XCII, CXII, CXXXV)

ezelī - Eternal in the past. (XVI)

Face - The vision of the Divine Beloved in Paradise. (XCV)

Fear and Hope - The true lover will have gone beyond fear of Hell and hope of Paradise. (XII)

fenā - Annihilation of self in God; non-existence.

ferej - A cloak worn by the religious class on ceremonial occasions. (CLXXXII)

Ferhād - The name of a famous lover in Persian literature, lover of Şīrīn; famous for undertaking to remove a mountain so that a river could flow in front of her palace. (I)

fetva - Official opinion on a legal matter.

Fountain of Life - The Fountain of Life was thought to be in a dark place. Thus the person who enters darkness is one who does not follow God's path but instead tries to find eternal life. (XCII)

four angels - Jibrīl, Mīha'īl, Isrāfīl, and 'Azrā'īl. (CLXXIV)

Four Books - The Pentateuch, the New Testament, the Psalms, and the Kuran. These books were divinely transmitted to the prophets Moses, Jesus, David, and Muḥammad, respectively. (CII)

Four elements - Fire, air, water, earth. (XL)

ġāzī - Fighter for the faith.

God/the Truth (Ḥaqq) - Often symbolized as the sea. (CLXXXVIII) *ḥadīth-i qudsī* - Sacred, or holy, tradition; any class of traditions that reveal words spoken by God, as distinguished from the *ḥadīth nabawī*, which transmits the words of the Prophet. (LXXV)

ḥāl - Mystical spiritual state. The *ḥāl* is a received state, as opposed to the *makām*, which is acquired. The *ḥāl* is by nature instantaneous. (LXXXIV)

Hallāj (Mansūr) - (d. A.D. 922) An early mystic who had an enormous influence on Islamic mysticism. He claimed to have reached union with the Divine Beloved. He became the symbol of the suffering martyr of love. He was executed for his famous statement: "anā'l-Haqq"—I am God, the Absolute Truth (Reality). After he was hanged, he was decapitated and burned, and his ashes were thrown into the Tigris. (C, CLXXXVI)

halvet - Retirement from the world for the purpose of devotion. (XI)

Hamza - Uncle of the Prophet, said to be very strong. In one of the legends about him, he was said to have been captured and carried off to the Qāf Mountains. In the end he succeeded in killing all his captors. He fell at the battle of Uhud. (I, CII)

havāle - Barrier (Şemseddīn Sāmī, *Qāmūs-i Türkī*). (LII)

"I know myself" - Refers to the *ḥadīth* "He who knows himself knows His Lord." (CLXVII)

İblīs - The Devil, Satan.

ilāhī - Hymn.

imām - Leader of prayers.

Ismā'īl - A son of Abraham whom Abraham was about to sacrifice until God sent down a sheep for him to sacrifice instead. (XL, C)

Isrāfīl - The Angel of Death who will blow the last trumpet. (III)

Jerjis - A prophet who came after Jesus, was killed by his tribe seventy times, and returned to life seventy times. (XLV)

Ka'be - The Kaaba in Mecca. The small, nearly cubical stone building in the court of the Great Mosque at Mecca. The Kaaba represents the direction (*qıble*) to which Muslims turn in prayer.

Kevser - A river in Paradise; for the *sūfī*s it symbolizes spiritual knowledge. (XXXIX, LV, CLXXXII)

Khızır and İlyās - Khızır, a shadowy figure mentioned in the Kuran, is in particular known as one who found eternal life. İlyās was said to have gone with Khızır and to have also found and drunk from the Fountain of Life. Once a year, on the morning of Hıdrellez (Khızır-İlyās) Day, they meet at a rosebush. Khızır helps those in trouble on land, and İlyas those at sea. (CLXXIII, CCII)

Glossary

Kun! ("Be!") - God's command that created the world. (CII)

lantern . . . of love - According to Alevī-Bektaşī legends, God created a lantern to be the holy light (*nūr*) of Muḥammad and Alī. (CIV)

Leyla and Majnūn - Two famous lovers from Arabian literature, main characters of a number of works in Turkish and Persian. The youth, Qays, falls in love with a girl, Leyla, and is so stricken by love that he is called mad (*mejnūn*). The two lovers die without achieving union. Majnūn is often used as the symbol of the totally distracted lover and the symbol of the lover who gave up all for God's love. (XL, CXCIV)

Manṣūr - See "Ḥallāj."

medrese - Traditional Islamic university.

Microcosm of the Whole - Man sums up the universe. He is connected both to the animal and to the spiritual world and reflects within himself the divine attributes. (C)

miḥrāb - The niche in a mosque indicating the *qıble*. (XI)

Mi'rāj - Muḥammad's Heavenly Ascent. (CIV)

miṣkāl zerre - A mote's weight; refers to Kuran 4:40; 10:61; 34:3, 22; 99:7, 8. (LXXXIV)

moon of the fourteenth day - The full moon, representing the ideal shape of a beautiful face. (LXX)

muftī - Expounder of the Holy Law. (XXXVI)

Münker, Nekīr - The two angels who will question the dead person about God, His Prophet, His religion, and the Book. (XII, XC)

mürşid - Spiritual mentor.

nāz - Literally, "whim," "unorthodox behavior." Gölpınarlı (*Yūnus Emre . . . Dîvân*) says *nāz* is one of the attributes of God's beloveds, who at times say and do things that appear inappropriate or unpleasant. The concept is based on the *hadīth* that says if God loves one of his servants, the servant's misbehavior or sin will not adversely affect him. (CLXVII, CCIII)

Night of Power - The night when the Kuran was revealed, the twenty-seventh of the month of Ramażān. (LV)

Nimrūd's fire - Refers to the story about idolators (whose king is traditionally called Nimrūd) who threw Abraham into a fire, but God made the fire cool. (C)

ninety thousand words - Muḥammad spoke this many words with God at the time of his Heavenly Ascent. Of these Muḥammad is said to have revealed thirty thousand to those of advanced spiritual understanding; another thirty thousand he is said to have hidden and to have spoken only among the *ṣūfī*s. (CIV)

142

Nūshīn-revān - Sassanian king of Iran in the sixth century. (IX)

parmak hesābı - Syllabic meter; reckoning a line's meter by counting on the fingers.

Pen - See "Tablet." (XLI)

Pharaoh (Fir'awn) - In Islam he is the prototype of pride, lust, and attachment to self. In Poem IX he is used as a symbol of a possessor of great wealth.

pretext - According to a *hadīth*, God created the world, and man in it, because He wanted to be known. Thus, man was created for the sake of God, who in turn created all for man. (XXIV)

qadīm - Sempiternal, eternally preexistent. (XVI)

Qāf Mountains - The high mountains believed to surround the world. (IX, CII)

qalem çalınmak - Gölpınarlı (*Yunus Emre . . . Dîvân*, p. 225) defines as "to write fate, what will happen (to someone)." (XLI)

Qārūn - Mentioned three times in the Kuran (28:76-82; 29:39/38; and 40:25/24). He was known for his great wealth. (IX)

qıble - The direction of prayer; the Kaaba in Mecca. (XI)

qıl ū qāl - Redhouse (1890), p. 1419, translates as "tittle tattle." (CCIII)

rebāb - A three-stringed violin. (XLI)

risāle - Treatise.

Rızvān - Name of the doorkeeper of Paradise. (CIV)

rust - Refers to the traces of material existence that becloud the heart's mirror. (VI)

scales and bridge - Refers to the scales that will weigh a man's deeds at the time of Resurrection and to the Sırāt bridge. See "Sırāt." (XII)

seven texts - The seven different ways of reading the Kuran. There are *hadīth*s that say the Kuran can be read in seven different ways without any change in meaning. The *sūfī*s believe these seven different ways yield seven different meanings (Gölpınarlı, *Yunus Emre . . . Dîvân*, p. 298). (CLXXXII)

seventy-two languages - Although there are seventy-two languages in the world, all have the same meaning. Kuran 23:51-92 states that the brotherhood of Truth is one. (XCIV)

Seydī Balum - According to one source he was a prince from the house of Germiyan, an early Turkish principality. This shadowy figure has also been associated with a very early religious figure, Geyikli Baba. (CLXXXVIII)

sheikh - Spiritual mentor.

sifat - See "attribute."

Ṣimurg - Means "thirty birds" in Persian. It refers to the mythical bird whose nest is in the Qāf Mountains. It is as large as thirty birds and is made up of thirty colors. For the *ṣūfī*s it symbolizes the ability of matter to take every form (Gölpınarlı, *Yunus Emre . . . Dîvân*, p. 288). (CII)

Ṣırāṭ - Bridge over Hell, leading from this world to Paradise. It is thinner than a hair, sharper than a sword. Misbelievers and evildoers will not be able to cross it and will fall into Hell. (XII, LXXXIV, CCIII)

Straight Path (*toġru yol*) - Translation of the Arabic *Ṣirāṭ al-mustaqīm.*

ṣūfī - Islamic mystic.

Süleymān - King Solomon. (IX)

Tablet, the - According to traditional belief, while God was creating the world, he created a large, green tablet and a great pen. God commanded the Pen to write, and it wrote everything that would happen up to the Last Judgment on the Tablet. The original of the Kuran was also inscribed on the Tablet. (XXXVII, XLI)

tāj - Dervish headgear. (CLXXXII)

Tapduk - Yūnus's *mürşid*, or spiritual mentor. (LV)

tarīqat - Dervish order.

tekke - Building where dervishes gather to pray, etc. (see n. 4 to the Introduction).

title of privilege - See "*berāt.*"

'ulemā' - The learned class, doctors of Muslim theology.

ümerā' - The ruling class.

vaqt - Time, the present moment, the moment a mystical state is granted to a *ṣūfī* (Schimmel, *Mystical Dimensions of Islam*, pp. 129, 130). The unit of psychic measure of the encounter, or its absence. (XI)

Venus (Zühre) - The star of musicians, also associated with pleasure and sensuality. (III)

xıyānet - Treachery, ingratitude, perfidy. The idea reappears over and over again in literature that the ungrateful person (to parents, to God, and, by extension, to His Holy law) is a terrible wretch. (XI)

zıkrullāh - Litany in praise of God, dervish religious service.

Selected Bibliography

In Turkish

Akbank Uluslararası Yunus Emre Seminer-Bildiriler. Istanbul: Akbank Yayınları, 1971.

Banarlı, Nihad Sami. *Resimli Türk Edebiyati Tarihi.* Ankara: Milli Eğitim Bakanlığı, n.d. Fasc. 5, pp. 325–36.

Gölpınarlı, Abdülbâki. *Yunus Emre—Hayati.* Istanbul: Ikbal Kitabevi, 1936.

_____. *Yunus Emre—Hayati, Sanati ve Şiirleri.* Istanbul: Varlık Yayınevi, 1957.

_____. *Yunus Emre—Hayati ve Bütün Şiirleri.* Istanbul: Altın Kitaplar Yayınevi, 1971.

_____. *Yunus Emre—Risâlat al-Nushiyya ve Dîvân.* Eskişehir Turizm ve Tanıtma Derneği Yayını 1. Istanbul: Sülhi Garan Matbaası, 1965.

_____. *Yunus Emre ve Tasavvuf.* Istanbul: Remzi Kitabevi, 1961.

Köprülü, Mehmet Fuad. *Türk Edebiyatinda İlk Mutasavvıflar.* Istanbul, 1919. 2nd ed. Ankara: Ankara Üniversitesi Basımevi, 1966.

Öztelli, Cahit. *Belgelerle Yunus Emre.* Ankara: Karaman Turizm ve Tanıtma Derneği Yayınları, 1977.

Saygun, Ahmet Adnan. *Yunus Emre—Soli, Koro ve Orkestra için Oratoryo.* Ankara: Doğuş Matbaası, 1957.

Şemseddīn Sāmī, *Qāmūs-i Türkī.* Istanbul: İqdām, 1901.

Timurtaş, Faruk K. *Yūnus Emre Divanı.* Tercüman 1001 Temel Eser. Istanbul: Kervan Kitapçılık Basın Sanayi ve Ticaret A.Ş., n.d.

In German and English

Birge, John Kingsley. *The Bektashi Order of Dervishes*. London: Luzac and Co., 1937.

_____. "Yunus Emre: Turkey's Great Poet of the People." In *The MacDonald Presentation Volume*. Princeton: Princeton University Press, 1933.

Gibb, E. J. W. *A History of Ottoman Poetry*. 6 Vol. London: Luzac and Co., 1900-1909; rpt. 1963.

Gibb, H. A. R., ed. *The Travels of Ibn Baṭṭūṭa*. Vol. 2. Cambridge: Cambridge University Press, 1962.

Halman, Talat S., ed. *Yunus Emre and His Mystical Poetry*. Indiana University Turkish Studies 2. Bloomington: Indiana University Press, 1981.

MacCallum, Lyman. "Yunus Emre." *Muslim World* 36 (April 1946).

Menemencioğlu, Nermin. *The Penguin Book of Turkish Verse*. London: Penguin Books, 1978.

Redhouse, Sir James W. *A Turkish–English Lexicon*. Constantinople: A. J. Boyajian, 1890.

Schimmel, Annemarie. "Drei türkische Mystiker: Yunus Emre, Kaygusuz Abdal, Pir Sultan Abdal." *Mitteilungen der Deutsch-türkischen Gesellschaft* 48 (1962).

_____. *Mystical Dimensions of Islam*. Chapel Hill: University of North Carolina Press, 1975.

_____. "Yunus Emre." *Numen* 8, fasc. 1 (January 1961).

Vámbéry, Hermann. *Čagataische Sprachstudien*. Leipzig, 1867. Reprint. Amsterdam: Philo Press, 1975.

Walsh, John R. "Yunus Emre: A 14th-Century Turkish Hymnodist." *Numen* 7, fasc. 2–3 (December 1960).